PRAISE FOR

EMBODYING THE GODDESS

"Cynthia Abulafia has lived with many forms of the Goddess throughout her life. In this book, she offers questions, stories and guidance inviting others along the path she has found. As a mother, yogini, teacher, and spouse—and most of all, a human being—she writes with kindness, humor, wisdom, and compassion for integrating transcendence and every day immanent life. Truly a valuable friend to have along the way!" —**Hallie Austen Iglehart**, author of *The Heart of the Goddess*

"This book invites a deep renewal of acquaintance with oneself. Through engaging philosophical principles, parables, and familiar, concrete examples, it celebrates ways of knowing the Goddess who already resides within us." —**Dr. Emily Lord-Kambitsch**, professor, Mythological Studies Program, Pacifica Graduate Institute

"*Embodying the Goddess* is a transformative journey into the universal goddess that resides in us all. This book beautifully reminds us to live from the heart—and of our innate strength, intuition, and connection to the sacred feminine." —**Julia Rockwell**, author of *Mothering Earth: The Busy Family's Guide to Saving the Planet*

"A beautiful book about the feminine approach to nondual awakening, which men interested in this subject will love too. Two things stand out in terms of realizing the goal of true inner freedom; first, we are either moving toward compulsion, with all its limitations, or open-hearted reverence; and second, curiosity is the most essential trait in self-inquiry, because it leads us to our true nature—peaceful, loving, and free!" —**Jim Dreaver**, non-duality teacher and author of *End Your Story, Begin Your Life*

"Cynthia's book is a lucid and powerful guide for those seeking the highest form of success: living a beautiful and just life. As a scholar of ancient traditions and a yogi, the author combines both academic rigor and embodied intuition to guide us closer to the truth of what it means to be alive at this moment in time. Being in her presence, reading these words, is in itself a profound form of healing, for ourselves and the planet." —**Flavia Maia, PhD**, Obama scholar, Dalai Lama Fellow, activist and founder of Filha do Sol, a woman led environmental initiative on the frontlines of climate change in Brazil

"*Embodying the Goddess* is a profound exploration of the divine feminine and a call to action for our personal and collective healing. A beacon for those seeking to understand the divine as a living presence within their own body, mind, heart, and everyday actions. Abulafia's deep reverence for the Goddess path, informed by her own experiences and extensive studies, makes this book an essential read and roadmap for anyone yearning to deepen their spiritual practice and embody the divine in every aspect of their lives." —**Richard Miller, PhD**, founder, iRest Institute and author of *Yoga Nidra: The iRest Meditative Practice for Deep Relaxation and Healing*

"What I find remarkable about *Embodying the Goddess* is Cynthia's combination of deep scholarly rigor and her exploration of the spiritual human experience. In a time when Yoga practices have become commodified, Cynthia's willingness to engage deeply with ancient texts and nuanced ideas is refreshing. She explores the complexities of embodiment, offering a rich intellectual framework, yet encourages the reader to move beyond words and into personal, lived experience—where the true depth, challenge, and vulnerability of this journey lies. These are tricky concepts to capture, but worth moving towards and examining nonetheless." —**Kaita Mrazek**, author, founder of The Listening Movement (TheListeningMovement.com)

EMBODYING THE GODDESS

HOW TO AWAKEN CURIOSITY AND REVERENCE ON THE SPIRITUAL PATH

CYNTHIA ABULAFIA

MONKFISH
BOOK PUBLISHING COMPANY
RHINEBECK, NEW YORK

Paperback ISBN 9781966608073
eBook ISBN 9781966608080

Library of Congress Control Number 2025037117
Library of Congress Cataloging-in-Publication Data Pending

Book and cover design by Colin Rolfe

Monkfish Book Publishing Company
22 East Market Street, Suite 304
Rhinebeck, NY 12572
(845) 876-4861
monkfishpublishing.com

For my family: Justin, Ayla, and Teo
and Life, which is the Breath of the Mother

Contents

Let me, like other people,
Yearn deeply for the objects of the world,
But allow me to view them as your form,
O Lord, without contradiction.
In the different stages
Of the growth of the body
In the modifications of the mind
In the many situations
On the path of life,
Reveal to me your own blissful form.
Let the sense faculties, full of delight,
Be attached to their respective objects.
But may there not be, even for an instant,
Any loss of the joy of your nonduality.

-Utpaladeva (Śivastotrāvalī, Stotra 8)

Introduction

I WAS SITTING down for lunch with a friend, Flávia, a leader in climate change activism from northeastern Brazil. Flávia is powerful and passionate, and also impressive. She stands at the frontlines of the climate crisis in one of the most at risk places in the world, a place where the mangroves are disappearing and the taps open, more often than not, to brown water. On this late spring afternoon in California, though, we weren't only talking about Mother Earth. We were talking about Mary Magdalene. Flávia shared a recent experience: "One night before going to sleep I asked Her to show me Her face in my dream. I had a dream where I walked by several women wearing colorful veils, and every time I lifted a veil I saw the face of a woman I know in my life—my friends, my family members. Under one veil I even saw my own face. I woke up with the sense that we are all Her, and she is coming to all of us through our own faces, bodies, and actions in the world."

When people find out that I study the Goddess, the stories start to come out. Slowly at first. A little shy and slightly tentative. Usually, we hide the stories. We hide the dreams, the prophetic whispers, the intuitions, and the visions. We know She's communicating but we wonder, *Who is She? What does it mean?*

We can start with who She is. She is embodied existence—our thoughts, emotions, sensations, perceptions, and memories. She is mother, matrix, and movement. All of Her representations point to Her being-ness, which is embodiment. The sole aim of this book is to answer, "Who is She?" thoroughly enough to directly access existence as embodied infinity. As for, "What does it mean?" The Goddess is waking up. That's what it means. The Goddess, however we know Her culturally and metaphorically, is coming to us—in dreams, in whispers, in community, in meditation. She is in that hard conversation with a friend who needs to process. She's on the frontline where spiritual crisis meets climate activism. She is in the voice of people who want a different way of connecting, communicating, or inhabiting their experiences. She is in our intimate and closest relationships. She is in our therapy, psychology, trauma work, and empowerment projects. She is in our desire to turn toward our complicated bodies, our complicated lives, and our intuition.

But before She can appear in the world, or even in support of our personal and collective healing work, She must first become established in our hearts. When the Goddess taps us on the shoulder we must listen so that we know what She is communicating to us. She is walking us through forests and fields and showing us the way into ourselves. I call this the *Goddess path*.

I want to remind you how to walk Her path. Being one who loves Her doesn't mean holding the Goddess *apart* from yourself or revering Her in external things. That will happen, too, because you will start to see Her everywhere. But we get to that by falling in love with ourselves first. We only truly revere the external by becoming anchored in the internal. We remember the Goddess in our hearts and we become Her. Then we look through Her eyes.

This isn't possession or romantic projection. It is not a soft, sweet, saccharine surrender. Becoming the Goddess means falling in love with everything—the light and the beauty as well as the dark, pain, rage, stupid, or ironic. She can't just be one thing. She has to be the whole of it.

The divine feminine operates, as we will see, on the deep inner pulse. The pulse is expansion and contraction, going out and coming in. Heartbeat and breath. When we are following the path of the Goddess we learn to listen for the pulse in all things. In the world of pulse, we are only ever deepening into reverence or we are living in compulsion. It is that simple. That's what this book says over and over again. We get to know our compulsion and our reverence by awakening our curiosity. How compulsion and reverence play out in the world is not very simple, until we see the single pin—curiosity—that holds together the bigger pattern. Until we learn how to fully reclaim the agency of our hearts. Until we learn to listen to all of the layers of ourselves. We need the tools to really get it. This book is about learning, step by step, or layer by layer, how to deepen into reverence.

We have been unwise. We have agreed to stories and acts of madness and we have been injured. We can change this. Changing is the gift of following reverence over compulsion, or learning to be wise. We can stop making injurious contracts that will only lead to pain and shame when we bring the Goddess back into the fold of our being. We put the power back on ourselves.

The twentieth-century mystic and teacher Nisargadatta Maharaj said, "I do not see a sufferer, I am the sufferer.... I follow no rules nor lay down rules. I flow with life, faithfully and irresistibly."[1] I hear the Goddess in these words. In practical terms, I consider myself a weaver. I don't stand at a podium and sit facing the crowd, delivering my wisdom from the top-down or from the singular to the multitude. I am not a perfected being. Far from it. I cry. I pray. I get stuck. I dig deep, make mistakes, apologize, get curious, and do it all again. I sit elbow to elbow with stories and sisters and brothers and silence and thrum, building the fine webs of thread through countless bodies and hearts so that my curiosity, like a bright electric current, can spark around, through, beyond, and within myself and others.

Weavers can see patterns. I can get above the ground high up enough to see the shape and color of the fabric that's being woven around me, through me, and by me. I know which path leads to which place. This is my skill. I'm not good at many things (ask my kids), but

I do have this one thing. I have always been able to see the structure of things.

The structure can create a guide. That guide is for you to walk. You must be your own weaver, creatrix, and lover. What you do with the creative unfolding is your choice—that's your Goddess path. It is not my job to guide the narrow straits or the hidden valleys, only to name and describe them so that you can have a heads up. So that you can move with reverence and transmute the compulsion, dullness, stagnation, or disassociation that may be armoring your heart. I am walking that path alongside you.

I am a long-time devotee of the goddess Kālī, who came to me nearly twenty years ago through a series of energetic awakenings (what is sometimes called *kundalini awakening*) that started when I was a young child and culminated in a massive paradigm shift in my early twenties that is still echoing and deepening in my body today. I did not choose Kālī. She chose me. I loved Her the way a young child loves a mother. And like a child, I threw many temper tantrums and tried to thrash in Her embrace. I got mad at Her. Sometimes I wanted Her to go away. She never went away.

She communicated to me directly for over a decade before She showed me Her image. Then, one day, I saw a painting of Her and stopped in my tracks, "My god. It's *Her*." To be honest, when I did finally see Her image, I felt a sense of total relief. But I also rolled my eyes. "Of course She hid Herself." Typical. Now I was the annoyed teenager. It was well over a decade of experiencing Her directly before I cracked any books about Her, or heard any sacred sounds associated with Her, or knew about Her representations in image, geometry, or myth. I experienced Her in my body before I put on that piece of jewelry called *study*.

Now I study this particular Goddess in Her "home court"—in the traditions that named and mapped Her. Because She has me by the tail, so to speak, I frame the Goddess path mostly through these traditions. I particularly love the tantric or shakta traditions. These Goddess-centered traditions are some of the most beautiful, developed, and detailed spiritual maps ever created—developed primarily in the early medieval period of the common era.

You'll notice little marks on some of the words associated with these traditions (like Māyā) called diacritics. They help us properly pronounce a word in another language. In this case, most of the words with diacritics that I use are the romanized form of Sanskrit. When they are used to name a Goddess, I always keep them. In other cases, like book titles or other Sanskrit words, I may leave the marks off. Words that are very commonly used in the west (shakti, prana) do contain diacritics, but I omit them for the sake of easy reading. I only capitalize "Her" and "She" to name the Goddess in the introduction so as to introduce and honor Her, but then leave the formality off thereafter.

Psychotherapist Abraham Maslow said, "We fear to know the fearsome and unsavory aspects of ourselves, but we fear even more to know the godlike in ourselves." This book is my way of exploring the godlike (or, as it were, the goddess-like) in ourselves. In the first part I explore what I mean by the Goddess path, and why it's important for us to remember Her, metaphorically and structurally—if not also literally. History is a valuable anchor for this plea because history reveals just how much we humans have always loved Her, until we forgot. I start by exploring *what* She represents, *why* we forgot, and *how* we forgot. Much of prewritten history must be inferred through archeology, anthropology, and a good amount of reading between the lines of sacred texts—especially the earliest ones that were collated. I cite some of these resources and explain them where I can.

But it's not enough to make a plea on behalf of the Goddess for spiritual embodiment. There has to be a way to do that. The second part, and the bulk of this book, is therefore a guide into and through the layers of the heart. The Goddess path is about reorienting us to live from the heart. To do this I offer a model created by my favorite teacher, a mystic genius named Utpaladeva who lived in northern India over 1000 years ago around 900 CE. He describes the heart as simultaneously physical, thought-emotional, intuitive, and transcendent. Once we understand how to identify and celebrate these layers, we might radically reorient our understanding of ourselves. We must reclaim all of our layers. Once we do, we can enter into the the living embodied practice of playing our essential layers harmoniously. This is sometimes called the saturation layer, or beyond-the-transcendent. We can call it integration.

The third part of the book offers a description of what it looks like to fully embrace the Goddess in the day to day. This section offers a practical description of integration. Because She plays in the field of embodiment—the things we can touch, see, hear, and feel—this final section includes a fresh perspective on how we can relate to others and to ourselves with reverence. Since She is life, movement within the transcendent, it's delightful to dance with Her in these human perceptions. Relationship and communication helps Her. Turning toward the complex wakes Her. Excavating the muck ignites Her.

You may wonder why I have made use of the female gender in this spiritual book, which after all, is a book about embodying your life (no matter what gender, sex, race, ethnicity, or type of life form you happen to be). This is not to create another binary or gender normative trope for some "Goddess archetype" to fill. I could easily use the term "embodiment" instead of "the Goddess," and as a teacher and workshop leader I do in fact use that more neutral term frequently.

However, I hope you understand as you read further why the Goddess is such an important framework for embodiment, especially when speaking about a spirituality that has carried and perpetuated what I call the *transcendence bias*, a key aspect of religious and philosophical patriarchy, for several thousand years. Naming Her as the embodied one does work in many ways, and it holds a historical precedent through many spiritual traditions, which we will see. So my desire to frame embodiment as the Goddess addresses multiple needs: it is an act of bringing agency back to the embodied and complex aspects of our being. It is a reignition of the sacred feminine in a way that is clearly visible, well-represented, and planted firmly on this earth in this time. Mother Earth needs many priests and priestesses who are well aware of their spiritual roles in service of the divine feminine.

But mostly, as a student of Hers (sometimes more and sometimes less willingly), I hope that you fall in love with Her totality—with yourself, your dear ones, your process, and with your heart—as much as I continue to fall in love with my own heart day after day, year after year, slog after slog. This is not a path with an end or a goal. It is a deepening spiral. Let's dance that spiral together.

PART ONE

MOTHER IS CALLING

CHAPTER 1

Embodied Spirituality

WHEN I WAS young, I used to play a game where I would stand at one end of a room and then run halfway to the opposite wall. Then I would run halfway again. I would do this for some time. It wasn't as exciting as it sounds. If you had walked in and observed me, chances are I would be squatting and staring very intently at a small space right up against that opposite wall, trying to figure out how to get to the wall, which of course I never could.

We are fascinated by infinity. We are also fascinated by edges. The two contradict one another in a way that we all understand so profoundly that children and brilliant physicists alike take notice. We are at odds. We experience the infinite within ourselves but we also experience the limited. The profoundly large lives within us, and so too does the very small. In one way or another, every spiritual religion and tradition tries to reconcile this. Where do I end? Where does the space around me begin? Limitation crash lands on the infinite. When these two aspects of the human experience butt heads we call it *suffering* or *spiritual crisis*. This crisis does not happen because we carry both but because we have prioritized only one of these experiences, the infinite, over the other.

It is the job of spirituality to reconcile our turmoil. Spirituality should invite deep peace by reuniting the many parts of the human experience into one profound whole, and yet it is in the spiritual traditions where the human experience has become the most biased. We have, gradually and over time, stepped more and more on the part of the scale that explores silence, stillness, and salvation *from* life. We have almost entirely forgotten the embodied experience. The weights are broken. Our hearts are unbalanced, and in trying to hold on, we've become very rigid. We are so out of balance that we cannot even remember what it is like to feel whole.

God and the Goddess

In order to understand the Goddess path, we need to understand who she is and where she excites. She stands on the part of the scale that invites experiential life. All of it—the mysterious, the awful, the glorious, belongs to her. In order to rebalance the heart, we need to understand how we have systematically created biases within ourselves to diminish, oppress, and subordinate what the divine feminine represents. We have done this in nearly all of the corners of our minds, even though she holds the key to integrating all of the opposites, all of the complexity, that we carry.

It can be painful to come back to the Goddess path because she represents the complex rather than the linear. We have a lot of voices in our heads. We have doubts as well as certainties. We feel unworthy but also connected. We feel afraid and also bold. We may have become spiritually arrogant by becoming fixed on concepts or roles. Sometimes we're in physical or emotional pain. Walking her path confronts us with opposites: how we can hold grief and joy at the same time, how agitation and peace share the same bed, how our smallness and our vastness dance in sweeping arcs around the rooms of our bodies. When we see these opposites we see what hurts and what's hidden, the little notes we have written to ourselves, the contracts we have made to protect ourselves against life, the children that live inside of us with their unvoiced experiences, all tucked up and folded tight and then placed someplace deep, into some hidden nook of the heart or behind an aching unstretched wing.

The Goddess is life, which means that she is the paired opposite of death. She plays in forms, like body and sound vibration and the dancing cosmos. One of the earliest religious texts came from Sumer, part of Babylon, before 2500 BCE. It clearly honors the Goddess as foundational and primary, calling her, "The Lady of Birth," and "The Great Good Queen of Heaven." An inscription reads, "When she speaks, heavens shake. When she opens her mouth, storms roar."[2] As life, she lives everywhere, in and as all things. All images are hers. All sound is her. All movement is her.

Whatever we call an object is her. This is built into how we address her. The article we fold into her name tells us a lot: *the* Goddess is usually an object, whereas God is a subject. A subject is singular. God. This is the observer, the witness, and the stillness. The subject does not require an article—he is simply God. The object is multiple, can be observed, and has shape, form, and vibration. The Goddess is many things. She is "the..." followed by all things. The—*everything*.

So in Love that She Creates Herself

This all powerful divine feminine is remembered in certain Goddess traditions out of India called *Shakta* traditions, sometimes called "tantra." The word Shakta comes from the word "shakti," which means energy, flow, or life. The term is feminine and sometimes refers explicitly to the Goddess. "Tantra" refers to a kind of spiritual text within a kaleidoscope of initiatory traditions.

It is important to note here that those who practiced tantra traditionally did not refer to themselves as "tantrikas," as we often hear today. In the original terminology, a devotee on this path would have called their own tradition a *path*, such as the "mantramārga," or the *path of mantra* (empowered sound). While I only refer to a very specific set of traditions under the huge banner of tantra called Non-dual Kashmiri Shaivism, Trika, or Shakta traditions, I will nevertheless use the generalized term "tantra" here because it is a common, modern convention. I understand that it is a misunderstood term that is widely appropriated. I refer to these traditions frequently. I believe that the way that these traditions understand the Goddess is particularly beautiful and thorough.

Here is what tantra says: the Goddess is so in love with her beloved, with the God of total stillness and transcendence, that she creates herself out of stillness in order to give him the only thing that he does not have, to do the only thing that he cannot do. Infinity cannot bind itself. So that's what she does. She creates limitation as an act of wild freedom and love *so that she can give herself back to the infinite*. She is logically and practically impossible because the infinite cannot be bound.

And yet here we are: bound (most of us, most of the time). I know it and you know it and every person on earth with a body feels some degree of individuation. Even the truly transcended masters who live much of the time in a state of dissolution wake up in the morning, chew and swallow food, and get tummy aches once in a while. Even the enlightened masters have some sense of body, form, hand, foot. Everyone alive is dancing her impossible dance.

Understand that her freedom is not in her capacity to be infinite. She emerges out of the infinite, and so she's already that. But she is more than infinity. Her freedom is in her capacity to be finite. To be complex. To be limited. To be *form*. She is far more powerful than the infinite. Her power lies in her freedom (in tantra, this type of freedom is called her *svatantrya*) to create a pulse, a vibration, a form, a this-and-that, a boundary, out of transcendent consciousness.

She ripples, turns, and flashes in and out of space and time. She pulsates. She is the stopping point on the infinite path, the places we halt and jolt and turn and try to pierce. She is you. She is me. Whatever gender, form, or sexual orientation–she is that. The feeling in your heart right now. For thousands (probably tens of thousands) of years she was the highest divinity respected by human societies because humans have always understood that life is circular, mysterious, full of multiformity within the unbounded sky of awareness. Usually, they honored her with natural principles like mountains or trees.

In the Bible we find the remnants of a deep, widespread, enduring worship of trees, possibly the ash tree or date palm, as the goddess Asherah, of her "poles," "sacred pillars," "wooden images," and her sacred sites "on every high hill and under every green tree." Later authors scrubbed her from the scriptures and called her followers "idolaters," "prostitutes," or "whores." They would not have been so harsh in their language if she were not such a formidable and well-loved form of the divine. She was powerful and pervasive. She was the tree and the mountain. She sprang up out of earth, offered the experience of life and creation of the living thing, and then reabsorbed that life back into her body. She was the womb of birth and the tomb of dissolution.

She is Goddess because women have the capacity to create new life. The female sex, at least in humans and most observable creatures, creates life out of her own body, expels that life, pushes and screams, nourishes that life with sweet milk, reabsorbs and heals her body after splitting open. She knows how to bleed, how to transmute, how to raise life, how to die.

As Hallie Inglehart Austen sums up in *The Heart of the Goddess*, "The Goddess represents a unity and wholeness which is the birthright and potential of every human being. All of us, all of existence, are the Divine. In order to complete this whole by bringing back that which has been denied, I name the Divine the Goddess."[3]

In modern spiritual tradition the Goddess is either not discussed at all, or she is psychologized as an archetype or she is something merely to overcome—that silly dream called life—on a path to what's *really real*, God. In monotheistic religions she is outright dangerous when she expresses her creative freedom. In some Indian traditions, like certain schools within orthodox Brahmanism and Vedanta, she is considered the source of all suffering, a hindrance. She is the dream of limitation that tricks us (see my exploration of Māyā in chapter 11). In these spiritual traditions the body and its activities are considered polluted, impure, and disgusting. This passage ascribed to the Sage Dattatreya in the Avadhuta Gita (ninth-tenth centuries CE) sums up one such attitude:

> Those who desire
> To acquire this eternal bliss and
> Of communicating it to others
> Through their teaching,
> Must give up all sensuous pleasures
> More especially those
> Which arise from sexual union.
>
> The body is made up of impure elements,
> Of blood, flesh, bones, and the like.
> Woe to those
> Who are attached to it,
> And indifferent to the ever blissful Self (7.13-14)

In my lifelong study of mythology, religion, and tradition, I have seen the infinite, described most often as Absolute Stillness (God, "the Self," etc.), highlighted above and beyond the finite in nearly every corner of human spiritual thought, belief, and philosophy. Infinity is better. Stillness is more real. Stillness is "Truth."

If you find it to be great fun to follow spiritual content on social media as I do, you will see all kinds of people posting insights, spiritual ritual, practices, and other offerings. No matter how ancient and traditional or how sincere and innocent these practices are—the young Brahmin boy learning to chant the Vedas, the young monk wearing his robes and following his teacher—you will invariably find someone in the comment section saying, "None of this is true. There is only Absolute Truth. Why make the child do this? Only stillness is real."

The Transcendence Bias

The transcendence bias states, "Only stillness is Truth." The transcendence bias has created a lot of problems for us because by loving a God without the Goddess we have put stillness and silence on a pedestal in most of the religious traditions, practices, and wisdom teachings born of the last three thousand years.

This spiritual bias underpins what I consider the *patriarchy of spirituality* and uses hierarchy models, calls out end goals, and uses militaristic analogies, metaphors, and concepts. Things, even souls, can be lost or won. When the God of the Old Testament is angry, he will urge the mass murder of all men, women, and children in a land he disfavors (for no apparent reason whatsoever), and he will call that "righteousness." It can get pretty grim. Murder is fully on the table as a viable and frequently used means in the patriarchy of spirituality.

On subtle levels the transcendence bias also relies on murder, but it usually uses different terms. Here is what this bias tells us in very common words: "Limitation holds us back from our freedom." "The unreal shields the real." "Let it go." "Be the witness." Death and stillness—these are the principles of patriarchal religion. Cut, release, transcend.

The Goddess says other things, but not these things. If you're thinking to yourself, *But that describes every single spiritual and religious tradition I know!* you're probably correct. This bias shows up everywhere. We don't even know there's another way. These are residues embedded inside of us from many generations of indoctrination, so much so that we have learned we must get very quiet if we wish for freedom. Not to dance wild in the moonlight, as our ancestors did, but to sit very still. So still that we go beyond the body.

It's no wonder that sacred death is honored as one of the highest achievements in religions and traditions that follow this model. In the transcendence bias, certain traditions sanction spiritual suicide, which began in early sects of Jainism and spread to Buddhism and other traditions, endorse spiritual death by abandoning the body, or they will reach for a state of salvation after death, often called Heaven.

We have been worshiping the *death principle* as God since Vedic and Abrahamic times, and the *life principle* has become feared, repressed, and even denied. It's absurd. And it's embedded in our spiritual speak, even in the most basic statements and assumptions that we make. I often call the transcendence bias "let it go" spirituality. It's everywhere. The "let it go" model gets mixed up into all kinds of traditions, even some of the traditions that we might call Goddess traditions.

We don't even hear ourselves saying it most of the time: "I should let this go." We just know we should do it. What does it even mean to "let it go?" Where is this "it" even going? And who is letting it "go" there? I know I have felt the dueling swordsmanship that Absolute Truth creates when only *stillness* is real. Perhaps you've tried to "let it go," and then, totally perplexed, said, "I have no idea how to do that." If you have succeeded in "letting it go," is that because you actually just—poof!—dropped the "it," or did you instead turn toward, investigate, chew on, digest, and absorb the "it" to such a degree that you did not have to think about it anymore because it was assimilated into your (now wiser) being?

Perhaps you have learned about non-attachment, tried to be a good student, and then been tugged away sharply by a family emergency, a pet that needed attention, or an important work call. Non-attached, until life knocks on the door.

The Transcendence Hangover

The death experience does matter when it is balanced. In the same way that we need a satchel to hold our grains, or we need a body in order to feel the pulse of the heart and the breath, and the banks and the bed of the river to hold the water, we need the touchpoint of death to reorient us back into life. God is very useful in this way. Stillness is the ground on which movement dances. We must make use of the infinite in the form of stillness. Usually in spiritual tradition a human direct experience that recognizes the infinite is a *transcendent experience*. This is a good thing and a sign of spiritual success. A transcendent experience is when we go beyond the limited individual and saturate into stillness. We leap past the edge of the body, past the edge of the page. We cascade over the waterfall at the end of the earth and find a vastness that cannot be described.

In the best possible way, this is a death experience. This death is usually welcomed—a release of a limiting notion or habit or belief or sense of self. There is power in a transcendent experience. Much has been written about it, and nearly all religious and spiritual models pay great respect to the transcendent aperture. Transcendent experiences are mystical and life-altering noetic reorientations that tend to change us and our perception of the world completely. In the dissolving of everything there is clarity. There is insight in death.

But reforming and coming back together into life is powerful, too. The high of the transcendent experience requires the come-down of the imminent—the landing home and the coming back into the individual to some degree. This is the, *Oh shit I'm me again* moment. When we do not acknowledge this part of the experience then the transcendence hangover is *real*. Coming back to the individual can hurt. One friend looked around at our beautiful seaside town after a transcendent experience and said to me, "After that, all this just looks like a cesspool." Like any hangover, the transcendence hangover can put us flat on our backs. Oh, it hurts to go from the very big, to the very small.

Of all spiritual phenomena, I find the transcendence hangover to be the least understood. Of all lessons it holds the greatest wealth for us, and yet we throw away the opportunity or become embarrassed or sad when we lose the transcendent state and become ... ordinary. Until one day we ask, *Wait, what is ordinary anyway?*

It is the job of the Goddess to guide us through the hangover because that's kind of her thing. It is her most potent power in action. This is where we see her wink at us. She is the life principle reforming itself. This is where she can hurt the most if we've pushed her away, but it's also where we can find the most reverence for her when we hold her close. It is the place where she breaks us open into our hearts.

The Mesoamerican goddess of the agave plant, Mayahuel,

represents this power. The agave is a spiral plant with razor sharp and knife-like leaves that move outward in all directions. If you have ever walked past an agave and accidentally (or purposefully) reached out your hand to touch it, you will get a sharp reminder of her prick. Mayahuel contains, in some accounts, four hundred breasts, each full with life's milk. The dangerous, razor sharp, the real, and the life-giving breast, flowing with milk. Let us not forget that as the goddess of the agave, the goddess associated with a plant that can create elixirs of pulque, mezcal, and tequila, she also nurses us into the mystical and altered experience.

Mayahuel fits all of the markers of how I see the complex dance between transcendence and life. To me she showcases the potential of the transcendence hangover. She carries danger and sustenance. She transports us into intoxication, and she has a form that is to be respected and that requires absolutely sober focus. She holds the mystical experience and she transmutes. There is frustration but also immense power in the thickening and condensing of the individual out of the cosmic, because it is in the creation of an individual out of the infinite that we begin to understand the wholeness that we fundamentally are.

It is not the transcendent experience that holds the key to life, but the return from transcendence. The contraction. The sharpening. The pulling into life that we have seen. The small-making. The sadness of going from infinitely big to small and strange. Again, we come back to opposites: we are vast, but we are bound. If we can follow this transition carefully, over and over again, then we will understand what freedom really means.

Compulsion or Reverence

My husband, a middle school science teacher, once mentioned that all raindrops and snowflakes rely on dust in the atmosphere in order for the water droplets to bind to something and then fall to earth. I clapped in joy when I heard this. *What! Rain can only fall once it gathers around dust?!* The water needs the dirt for structure. We also, like water, need to be able to wobble and collect around that little dirt speck in order to splash into existence and create all of life on earth. Without a tiny bit of dust the water is just too *watery*. There is a balance between structure and wobble, updraft of earth and downpour of rain, the play of opposites that allows everything around us to exist.

On the Goddess path we start to see that in the complex interweaving of the individual we have two choices at all times. We are either moving toward compulsion or moving toward reverence. Compulsion is a kind of rigidity. It's when the water of our being loses its wobble. Rigid things are brittle and when they fall they do not bounce—they fracture or they shatter.

We need to keep some wobble and wild dance when we look at the Goddess. Limitation can create bounce and wobble, which is reverence, or limitation can solidify and lose its curiosity—it can get brittle and rigid. Limitation is not only the body, which starts somewhere and ends somewhere (at least we believe that at first). Limitation also includes thoughts, emotions, sensations, perceptions, and memories.

We live in a complex time and the earth needs to be acknowledged. The mess needs to be seen. We need to learn how to wobble again, like the raindrop and like the snowflake. We need to get big and get small. We need to closely investigate transcendence when it arises and also when it slips away and condenses. We need to pay attention to the body. We need to listen to the earth. We need to bring back reverence. Limitation may even, just possibly, become more important and vital to us than absolute stillness. We are, after all, alive, and living things tend to jiggle. The weather is a constant wobble of all the elements. The elements never stop pulsating. Reverence shimmers.

By turning toward flow we will remember how to step into the role of the priest or priestess to the Mother. This book does not argue with the transcendent that can be touched directly by every one of us. I take the stillness aspect of the infinite to be a fact. I have touched transcendence many times. I bet you have too, for all of life dances with transcendence. It is an aspect of the infinite and it is the divine God principle. I bow deeply to that. It is a layer of reality and we will give it credit where it is due. Transcendence is waiting for us. We are all capable of touching the transcendent frequently and with depth.

However, I take it to be not an endpoint of inquiry, but a starting point. Stillness starts things. We are born from it, and we return to it. Stillness holds things. It is between all thoughts and surrounds all sound. Stillness saturates things. Enough of us have touched directly that infinite within, the recognition of total stillness and silence that forms the core of our being.

Stillness, when embodied, is form. Not just parts of you—the wise quiet one that wants badly to be the "best" inside of you, but *all* of you and your mess. I urge you to go further. To get a little rebellious, maybe even a little radical. I'd like to introduce you to a different way of seeing sacred embodiment, without being influenced by the transcendent bias that whispers, "Stillness is the only and highest truth." Sure, death is true. But life is true, too. The two are married, which is why we use the metaphoric terms "God" and "the Goddess," though you can use any other metaphor that you want: stillness and movement, transcendent and immanent. Religion has always gendered the two fundamental states, and I echo that language here because I like the metaphor and I think it has many layers. It has a history.

Beyond Archetype

The masculine and feminine play in all of us to varying and shifting degrees. In this place called life, however, we are in the realm of the Goddess because she has represented the form of things historically, metaphorically, energetically, and spiritually. We might as well use her convention while we understand how she works. Patriarchy was created and perpetuated where she was eliminated or crowded out. Ultimately, it is in life that we can find the real joy, the real freedom, and the abiding mystery.

Moreover, I don't only refer to the Goddess as an archetype. In the past hundred years when we began to yearn for her, we started to bring her back in this way, especially by men in academia and philosophy. She became a tool of psychoanalysts—the Athena archetype or the Isis archetype or the Kālī archetype. Again, we put her in her place and gave her a bit role.

But nowadays people are talking about the Goddess. A lot. We know she's been missing and we need to bring her back. We keep issuing invitations. As we try to coax her back into place, we call out and give her credit for all kinds of things.

We call her fierce. She fights for us.

We call her nurturing. She cares about the earth and the sovereignty of the natural home.

We bow to her as the seat of the creative, birthing life from her very body.

We call her destructive. She clears things out of our way using messy means like wind and rain and really bad breakups or really difficult family members.

We call her the one who integrates our experiences and heals us, the one who gives lessons, and the one urging us to make use of our traumas by sourcing the deep nectar of wisdom that is found in the challenge.

She is both/and, that is both fierce and nurturing, both creative and destructive. Calling the Goddess an archetype is one truth, but without the whole truth, calling her an archetype diminishes her. She represents the patterns of life. Yes. She represents *all* of life. More yes. I don't hate that she has been designed into archetypes—at least, not all of the time. But it is frustrating because it's another way to limit her. These are beautiful and honorable designations, but I would argue that all of these things are still one step removed from the real power at the core of the Goddess.

Even to say that we must "gain wisdom" from our challenges is not quite her, though we are close enough in that work to feel her breath on our necks. We can hear her jewelry reverberating in the process of learning from the challenge. We can feel the sweep of her clothing when we investigate closely our human pain and the stories and the relationships that we chew over time and again. We can smell her perfume and feel the closeness of her heat in the human experience. But to understand the Goddess, to see her, is to step into her body totally and let her senses become our own. This means that she is not quite the one that helps us move through our life and is not quite the wisdom that comes from challenge. She is not the representation or the archetype, but rather the thing itself. She is life. She is the challenge. She *is* trauma, and she is also healing. She is the vibration in real-time that is experiencing and sensing.

Goddess archetypes are useful to some degree and they are fun. I use them sometimes (Mayahuel!). They say, *She is the pattern for this or that principle*. She is a pattern within the whole. But she is also the whole. She is not just the actor on the stage that represents this aspect of our inner nature or that tendency. She is the stage itself, the wind blowing through the curtains, the breath of audience members, the bugs in the ground under the production, there before the play started and there after the stage is broken down. She is the whole of movement that, once seen clearly, is indistinguishable from God.

In Buddhism there is a saying: "It's best not to start on the spiritual path at all. If you do start, it's best to finish it." The true path of turning toward the Goddess is not easy. Everything is fed to the fire where stillness and movement meet. Expansion and contraction. Inbreath and outbreath. Everything. Here we follow a map to our curiosity: power of will, deep intelligence, and directive action all put together.

We are here as a hymn to the Great Mother. No insight that you gain belongs to someone outside of you, not to a person, words on a page, or a well-worn concept. All insights that your heart receives are yours, created by and for you. My commitment to this path is not for the sake of an extraordinary state, goal, nor even some insight that may come. Those belong to you. I'm here to explore and celebrate reverence. This moment is her—giving herself back to herself by creating and reabsorbing all-that-is, including limitation and challenge. As a devotee of the Mother, the great Goddess called life, destruction, time, and the will that gives birth to action, I bow to that movement and give myself entirely to her. She requires nothing and takes everything. Make sure you want to step on this path totally, because once you take that step, like the Buddhists say, it's best to finish.

A Practice

1. **Notice What You Notice.** Close your eyes and listen to the pulse of your body. You have a heartbeat. Your skin pulses, especially around your hands, belly, and your skull. Notice that you breathe in and out. Notice where you habitually hold tension, and notice where you are relaxed.
2. **Identify Compulsion.** Compulsion gets woven into our being so tightly that it takes time to unpack. This is not a race. Unpacking compulsion is the work of the whole lifespan. Be kind to yourself. Just notice if you're tight somewhere. Notice if you think you deserve to be tight, to not relax your breath into the bottom of your lungs, or if you use your legs to hold your body up. If you are sitting, are your upper thighs gripping? Can they relax? Can your spine hold you? Your spine is designed to hold you and it is perfectly capable of doing that. Once you let the top of your leg bone relax, try relaxing it again. Let the top of your leg bones drop.
3. **Identify Reverence.** Reverence is our most precious trait. Curiosity leads to moments of gratitude. Gratitude saturates and becomes reverence. Follow your curiosity into your body. Try to wind your way to your heart. If you start with your hands, follow your curiosity, then gratitude, then reverence through the pinky finger, into the deep inner arm, and back to your heart. Start to find these lines back to your heart and cultivate reverence.

CHAPTER 2

The Goddess Path

I HAVE AN ancestor who got himself into trouble with the pope. His name was Abraham Abulafia (1240–ca. 1291). After catching a glimpse of what he called "God's Mind," he became a well-known and vocal mystic, taking on ever stranger and wilder ascetic practices, staying in isolation, meditating, and chanting the sounds of his sacred text while making head movements. He used his body to communicate with God. He was a kabbalist, but a unique one with a different view from his peers. I've heard modern teachers call him the "Yogi of the Kabbalists."

At one point, Abraham decided that he needed to convert the pope, and so he walked barefoot to where the holy man was in residence outside Rome. The pope, not at all excited to have this wild rabbi tracking him down, ordered my ancestor's execution. But just as Abraham walked into town on that early morning, toward certain death, Pope Nicholas III died of sudden and mysterious causes. The sun rose. The sky lit. One man died. Another lived. My ancestor was spared.

Sources of the Goddess

I suppose I follow the family trait of walking into dangerous territory where the religious norm needs a good talking to. I follow the path of seeing things and then crossing dangerous boundaries, barefoot and determined, to exclaim them. The contrarian mystic has carried through the family for some 800 years. I am the daughter of a thousand rabbis. My father's fathers were rabbis as far back as he knows. My grandmother's family at one point held the largest Jewish library in the ancient world. Abraham lit a spark of rebellion, and I have turned that spark into a bonfire.

The threshold that I keep passing is in direct contrast, and sometimes in conflict with, both religious authority and spiritual dogma. Some people have gotten so used to these systems that they just won't want to hear what I have to say. Some people who already love her, who think they are a *part* of her, may get pushed to become *all* of her. When we talk about the Goddess, we have to do some surgery—some careful setting apart—and we have to do the suturing back together as well. She has gotten all mixed up with God. This requires organization. It requires undoing and redoing. It requires careful but certain movements.

We have to brush our hair until there are no knots left, until our hair glistens, until the comb passes through, before we can braid our hair. We need to understand the Goddess before she can be married, one and the same, in sacred marriage (*hieros gamos*), to God. She has been misunderstood. Her traits have been given to him. She has become confused in our minds. My job is ancestral and urgent. The mystic will show up strange and open armed to speak to your heart directly.

The Goddess was revered for tens of thousands of years—at least thirty thousand years through the Upper Paleolithic, into the Mesolithic (10,000-7,000 BCE) and the Neolithic Periods (7,000-3,000 BCE)—by the humans of this earth. She was the primary deity and overwhelmingly dominated religious symbolism in this vast timeframe. As Hallie Inglehart Austen notes, "The vast majority (over

90 percent) of human images from 30,000 to 5,000 BCE are female."[24] She represented birth, death (usually both at the same time), nature, things that turn in cycles, creation, destruction, and transmutation.

Her animal representations included the creatures of watery environments that so resembled the amniotic fluid of mother's womb, like frogs and fish. She represented nibbling goats and protective dogs. She sat flanked by two lions, and lions often sat protectively at her temple doors. Quite often she was represented by birds of prey, especially owls and other raptors, but also scavenging birds like vultures. For a long time she was depicted as a wild gorgon with large eyes and snakes for hair, leaving us Medusa as a final solitary representation of the ageless creature.

The bulls head, which looks so much like a uterus, was one of her visual symbols, and the bear and snake, with their cyclic regeneration—their hibernations and their sheddings and their mysterious emergences and transmutations out of yearly cycles—were her metaphorical symbols. In the Neolithic temples of Old Europe, ovens and looms have been unearthed inside the sacred chambers. In other temples, painted red, the structure was also the birthing chamber. The Goddess was celebrated through the acts of weaving and baking bread, giving birth and shedding blood. And why not? Of course, the most basic of our needs, to be clothed and fed, to be birthed and to bleed, must come from her and be her sacred act. That temples contained ovens shows that all transmutations—things that rise and take shape and change- belong to her.

Sometimes she had a husband. Usually, her husband was also her brother or her son. We see this motif—the Goddess and her lover/kin—in the remnants of history. She is Isis, Gaia, Hera, Sarasvatī, Asherah. Married to brother-son-father-husband. From the earliest times she was represented, amongst thousands of other symbols, as the downward pointing triangle. The triangle is the female sex organ, from which emerges all of human life, and by extension, creation itself.

When people began to engage more earnestly in warfare and social stratification, men and women lost their equality because men were needed to fight and women were needed to make more babies, ideally boys who would fight. This seeded the patriarchy. The author and journalist Angela Saini in her book, *The Patriarchs: The Origins of Inequality*, shows how this system may not have been dramatic or violent as some have argued but may have transitioned over time and space through shifts in customs, such as married couples returning to the home or town of the husband rather than the wife.

By the late Bronze Age, pastoral nomadic peoples began to settle from northern India to Anatolia, bringing their social stratification with them, including a male priestly tradition that could only be passed from father to son, from uncle to nephew. The famous, if sometimes controversial, twentieth century archeologist that described this transition in greatest detail, Marija Gimbutas, sometimes called these early people the Kurgan group, or the Indo-Europeans.

To this day scholars hotly debate Gimbutas' theories, some of which have stood the test of scrutiny, like her observation that early humans were Goddess-centered, creative, highly productive in skillful artistry, and that an influx of warrior peoples who rode horses and did not leave behind pottery or other skilled crafts came to dominate human history before 1,500 BCE. However, the invasions she imagined as abrupt and violent was likely a complex and more gradual process of assimilation. Gimbutas noted that many of the early male deities that came to dominate over goddess images during the Bronze Age stood on a mountain top and carried light- possibly originally representing lava, but morphing easily into the god bearing the lightning bolt (Thor, Zeus, and Indra), the sun (Aten), and the righteous god of light that fights against evil (Elohim, Yahweh, Allah).

In short, the timeless Goddess-worshiping religions that gathered around the sacred oven, baking bread, making sacred pottery, and weaving fabrics, were slowly transformed, wiped out, or absorbed into this new world order. After Christianity was accepted as the official religion of Rome in the early centuries of the common era, Roman law mixed with this new religion to solidify a patriarchy that was not only God centered but also extremely punitive and hierarchical. We still see the echoes of Roman civil law that infused religious law today. The man on the mountain—God—is still etched in our minds and our spiritual practices, and it's time that we see just how much spiritual real estate he takes up in our practices and worldviews.

Lineage Threads Woven in Time

Importantly, this God-on-a-mountain imagery in human history represented a broad shift to patriarchy, which includes patrilocality and patrilineality. In a patrilocal society a woman leaves her family home and moves in with her husband's family or to her husband's village upon marriage. When a woman leaves her ancestral home, a place where her own family is likely motivated to protect her, she often ends up alone and risks mistreatment or servitude in a foreign place. We still take on our husband's last names as a frequent custom in modern and progressive societies.

Patrilineal custom dictates that property passes from father to son or closest male heir. Throughout most of history the archeological records indicate that societies were commonly *matrilineal*: property was passed down from the mother to her daughter. This makes logical sense. We always know who our mother is, after all. Before humans understood the reproductive cycle, pregnancy and birth may have been considered a female act—a sacred dance between mother and spirit, or was at least the job of the female. The priestess honored creation and passed life through her body. Men were involved but in sometimes very creative ways that did not always reflect reproductive fatherhood.

In order for a society to be patrilineal rather than matrilineal, women had to lose some (or all) of their sexual freedom. If the father holds the family line, then he must have total authority over the female who carries and births that line. Sex and creation, now owned by men, in practical life meant that *women* had to be owned by men: they could not be equal, they could not hold positions of power and prestige, and they could not express sexual autonomy. Nakedness, once seen as natural, was no longer seen as natural. Sex, once a given right of expression by the Goddess, was now monitored and controlled. Virginity was cherished. Women could symbolically keep up the inner working of the house but they could no longer encircle the religious life of their peoples.

If the father holds the family line, then his god reflects him. He is no longer inclined to honor the Goddess of the hearth, the storyteller, or the old grandmother who keeps her family's collected memories. He is not inside the temple weaving and baking bread, but is instead outside, protecting what is his and holding his perimeter.

Not all at once, but over time and through the generations, the Goddess too fell. Her creative aspects now belonged to the male deities. Her transmutations, creation, and resurrection cycles were swapped with him—*he* now transmuted, *he* created, *he* resurrected. The Goddess as frog, fish, and bear began to disappear. The Goddess as snake was villainized. In the Bible, Adam created Eve out of one of his own ribs. In the Vedas, the Purusha (literally, "the man") was the first sacrifice, and his body was quartered into the highly structured caste system, dividing his mouth, arms, legs, and feet into the four social stratifications that largely remain in place to this day in India.

Women and men today, unless they come from the small pockets of wisdom traditions around the world that are not impacted by these patriarchal and patrilineal world views (and the last waves of colonialism and capitalism have erased most of those, too), hold certain biases in their religious and spiritual bodies that reflect this collective and ancestral swapping of roles.

We are due for a resetting of the table. We are due for a deeper, more radical equality. We need this not only for women but also for men, for how many of our sensitive and deeply feeling men have also been oppressed by a stern world that says "boys don't cry," and teaches him not to run to his mother past a certain tender age, barely up on his two little feet, lest he be called a "mama's boy" or a "wimp." We must excavate our most secret places of conditioning and correct what needs correcting. Men need to heal their mother-wound. Mothers need to heal their mother-wound. Girls need to heal their mother-wound. Planet earth, this great Mother, must be treated with respect once again. This healing has started in many ways in modern times and is still being done today, but we must do more to address the bias in current spiritual trends.

Curiosity Is Transparent

To do this, to heal the Mother, we will make use of the one thing we have, everyone and everywhere. We must get curious. Curiosity is almost the same thing as reverence. Curiosity is reverence *in action*—reverence in motion. It is reverence directed at the heart.

The Goddess, how I define her today, is our *awake curiosity*. She is the movement, the edges, and the boundaries (like the line in the room I chased, or our skin, or the space between this book and your fingers). Curiosity reconciles the transcendent model that builds hierarchies that move ever toward stillness and the absolute, with the experience of the Goddess, who turns upon a spiral where light and dark are undifferentiated, where the womb and the tomb coexist.

By untangling the hierarchies, we return to her that dignity which has been subordinated, countless times, in countless places, in countless traditions, and we women and men of the world reclaim our own wholeness of being in the process. Curiosity is the most essential tool that we, as humans stumbling toward the divine, carry on our life journey. When curiosity awakens, *we* awaken. Our power awakens. Waking up our curiosity not only brings us back to life but it also reignites our hearts, our souls, and our ability to listen ever more deeply to the subterranean aspects of ourselves- to the things that move way below the surface. Our intuition wakes up. Our knowing becomes more certain, but also more fluid. Our knowing becomes less jealous, less guarded, and begins to shake out of us, insistently, unapologetically, like laughter.

If I may be bold, and I hope you are willing to be bold too, I'd like to infuse curiosity back into your soul. I'd like you to observe directly and constantly how this life pours upon itself through us using this breathtaking trait of curiosity. We are born with it, and we can make use of it. Curiosity can be turned, cultivated, curated, dulled, directed, and repressed. It can be snapped shut when controlled. It can explode past the edges of the universe when unbounded. It can drive the body and spirit beyond what physical laws suggest are possible.

We can pretty much do what we want with our curiosity. That's because curiosity, as you might notice now, is transparent. Whatever curiosity touches is not colored by it. This is pretty rare. When grief touches something it paints that thing with grief. When happiness touches something there is a spark and a shift and an uplift. When we are angry in our hearts, we tend to be angry with the whole world. And yet, whatever curiosity touches is touched, felt, and noticed without changing that thing.

Curiosity is transparent. It can touch sadness, happiness, and other colorful states not only without diminishing them, but by deepening them and following their scent trails into tender and extraordinary places. This is how curiosity becomes our best tool in turning toward the complex, the opposites, that we carry. This is why curiosity is our best tool in psychotherapy, trauma work, and also in spirituality. It is, for this reason, the technology of the Goddess.

Why We Shut Down Curiosity

There are several ways that we shut down our curiosity. This is where the patterns, the archetypes, help us see things more clearly. One archetype that I find useful is the Athena archetype, described beautifully by Dr. Jean Shinoda Bolen, a Jungian and the author of *Goddesses in Everywoman*. Athena is the Greek goddess of wisdom and strategic warfare, as well as justice and order. She explains how it is often women who suppress the feminine the most fiercely. More than men, it is the wounded feminine that has done the most damage to her sex. Athena is born directly from her father's head, fully armored and fully grown. That tells us a lot. In all of the Greek myths this motherless and childless goddess, emerging from God's skull, stands up for the patriarchy, choosing the side of the male and punishing the female at every opportunity.

The Greeks—although we think of them as the underpinning of

reason and philosophy for the western world—were notoriously patriarchal. Women and slaves held similar positions in ancient Athens. The Athenian woman may be one of the most repressed females in history. Aristotle said that women were inferior to men and meant to be subjects. Before that, Hesiod- one of the earliest Greek poets and authors- said that all women were destructive.

When I find a woman who staunchly stands up for the patriarchy, who rallies behind the subjugation of her own sex, such as her right to manage her creativity, her physical body, or her working rights, I turn to this archetype and see her as an Athena. For example, Chinese foot-binding, where young girls broke the bones of their feet over and over again, so that they fit into shoes that were mere inches long, was a tradition held strong primarily by mothers and grandmothers. Movements tried to stop the practice for 1,000 years, but still mothers and grandmothers carried it on. It took the strict rules of communism (and Mao Zedong specifically) to finally stop the practice.

And then there's female genital mutilation in parts of Africa, the Middle East, and Asia, which involves the painful cutting or removal of the external female genitals, still practiced by over 230 million women. It is a practice that the women, mothers, and grandmothers keep alive because it is considered in many places to be a necessary and honorable way to raise young girls and to maintain their sexual purity. In these cases, as well as others, the female has lost her curiosity and towed to the strictest interpretation of her social order.

After the patriarchy was established, Goddess lineages were often feared, suppressed, or misunderstood by the mainstream. Our distaste for these traditions remains today, though for reasons far more complex than what I can cover here. The term *tantra* represents this point well. In medieval tantra women were allowed to join the Goddess lineage traditions and practices, and were particularly welcomed into Krama and Kaula. This is remarkable for a civilization where traditionally women could not join the priesthood, and in many orthodox communities, could not even listen to recitation of sacred chants, which were only for male ears. Foreigners, too, were often welcome in tantra, and so were lower class peoples. Any person with sincere curiosity and devotion could join. Religious success was not just for the aristocratic male.

Social norms were certainly challenged by this alone, but it gets better.

The path of the Goddess in recorded history shows determined challenges to social conditioning, to notions of purity and structure, including class and economic structure (no matter how rigid). This is scary and uncomfortable for a well-organized society. In some tantric schools, the vows of initiation included an absolute rejection of associating with the rigid social structures of birth, and some advanced practitioners, especially those associated with the Goddess centered Kaula and Krama lineages, engaged in sexual union for the specific aim of challenging that norm in two main ways.

In the first case, sex, the ultimate form of touch, between men and women of different social structures would have been deeply confrontational to social norms, dissolving any hidden hierarchies associated with social status remaining in the aspirant. Add to that the fact that the sexual fluids released in these sacred sexual rites, and other body fluids besides, were carefully collected and were then imbibed in the highest of ritual settings, indicating that all things are divine. Everything is divine, including menstrual blood. There would be no coming back to social norms around purity after drinking these human fluids in ecstasy and union.

The modern sexual freedom workshops generally known as "California tantra" (or neo-tantra) are her rebound, too, though we have appropriated all of these original sacred rituals for pleasure rather than for entering into the body of the Goddess. I don't know of any neo-tantra communities that collect and imbibe sexual fluids—yet. Still, an argument can be made that the neo-tantra practices are her social rebellion too because men and women have lived under the shadow of sexual prohibition, of the *good girl* and *nice boy* conditioning for so long. A lot of these new tantric approaches, though quite far from their namesake, are still in the spirit of awakening curiosity and bringing us back home to our bodies, our agency, and our whole creative expression.

The left-hand paths of tantra were a kind of counterculture in their day, and that counterculture has been picked up in the West in the past decades. Scholar Jeffrey Kripal notes that tantra "can also function as a perfectly accurate description of many of the metaphysical assumptions of the American-British counterculture, that broad band of utopian and mystical movements that arced between America and England in the 1960s and 70s and helped energize other more political projects, from civil rights, early feminism and the sexual revolution, to the anti-war and gay rights movements."[5]

Curiosity tends to go dormant in the well-structured and controlled, the organized and the injuncted. When curiosity is ignited in someone with intense focus it changes, moves, warps, moves rapidly on ladders of conditioning. Curiosity, when robust, has a way of getting us to dig, to turn in weird directions, to go for the root of things.

Curiosity follows the spiral, how it creates itself and reabsorbs itself. It sounds simple but it's heroic work. It is easily appropriated into the straight path with a goal. Fortunately, straight paths have a tendency to hit a turn now and then, and we remember, or we ask the questions that cause us to remember. Sometimes we get knocked right off our own paths and freefall into curiosity. My mother-in-law, after being a stay-at-home wife for decades, surprised the whole family by picking up pottery and clay throwing late in her sixties. For some reason her curiosity turned on and she took the dive. It became a tremendously beautiful art.

Where there is curiosity the Goddess path stands strong. There is no end to curiosity, and once we accept that curiosity leads us all the way down through the curving muck of human experience and the depth of the human heart, we can see that what it spotlights is worth the whole universe and beyond.

Goddess path principles are beginning to be taught and understood in the West, but usually disguised as therapeutic psychotherapy or psychology, as physics and science, or as occultism. We need to go further. Even in the East, these teachings have not been widely accessible. The lineages that have studied the Goddess have often faded away, only to crop up, coalesce briefly, or weave into other lineages altogether. Athena herself has disappeared into the history books, the mythology lectures, the books and musings of Jungian psychoanalysis.

If she, the Goddess, is the spiral then she has woven through history in just such a way as to come in and out of our awareness, to disappear altogether and then emerge, like a quivering particle in quantum mechanics that can only be tracked in probabilities and maybes, in a whole other place and time.

The Goddess path has diffused into a prism of directions in a million different ways, flickering out and then reappearing, the way a strong bonfire lets light dance in many directions, even way off into the pulsating distance. She is contained in the statement: "Movement is movement, stillness is stillness, movement is stillness, and stillness is movement. None of these and all of these." What a curious statement.

A Practice

Are you curious?

- Where do you feel your curiosity? Where is it open? What fascinates you?
- Where do you feel like your curiosity has been shut down? Where do you carry belief structures that were given to you by someone else: by your culture, society, or family? How does this impact your body?
- Was there something that made you curious when you were younger? What enthralled you? What did you want to know about the most? Do you still feel curious about that thing? Why or why not?

PART TWO

THE HEART

CHAPTER 3

At the Center of Your Being

RUMI SAID, "The truth was a mirror in the hands of God. It fell and broke into pieces. Everybody took a piece of it, and they looked at it and thought they had the truth." The mirror has been used as an analogy by many traditions over the millennia to describe consciousness, truth, and the heart. Let's see how the analogy helps us understand the Goddess, too.

The City in the Mirror

Think of life, including the body, as a whole and complicated network, everything connected, as the body of the Goddess. The body of the Goddess is kind of like a city. A city contains roads that lead to the temple, babies crying, children playing, people arguing, and people making love. There is a lot going on in a city, but it's still one dynamic whole, especially if we are looking at the city through the looking-glass.

At the center of our being there is a point of total stillness. But that stillness is somehow reflective, like a mirror. If life is the city in the mirror, the reflection, then that means that something is *emitting* that perception and then *receiving it* back again. Sometimes this reflective center is called the witness, the observer, or the "I am." In orthodox Brahmanism it is called Brahman, and in Vedanta it is called Atman. Tantra calls it the heart. This is a particularly useful term because we all know that the heart is inside of us. The heart is that origin, the birth place, the singularity from which everything radiates and to which everything returns. Life includes all of the reflections that shine back to the complex heart. Life, the Goddess, is the city in the mirror.

The life lived with reverence is the life that investigates the city in the mirror. The life that stays stagnant in compulsion ignores the mirror and carries on without stopping to take a look, or it only looks in the mirror when the compulsion is fishing for more compulsion-more of the same.

We all remember the wicked witch in Snow White who looks in the mirror, asking, "Mirror, mirror, on the wall, who is the fairest one of all?" When we already think we know the answer, or if our rigidity and our vanity say only one reflection is acceptable, then we will only be open to the image that we expect. Compulsion feeds vanity. This means that we may be trying to control the mirror. We lose our curiosity when we control the mirror. Like the witch in Snow White, we may become jealous and vindictive when the city in the mirror starts to show us images that contradict the compulsion and the control that we have carefully curated.

When the image starts to show painful things, we may have work to do. This can be scary and it can make us reactive. If my city is full of angry people and dark alleyways then I may not have a very fun time living in that reflection, so cleaning it up may be a good idea. There may be so much chaos in my city that I cannot even see that my heart is there at the center, emitting and receiving the images that I know so well and that capture my fascination. It might be that doing some clean-up work on the city streets is the only way for me to start to see the reflective surface that is emitting the content of my life.

Curiosity is a handy tool that can do that work for us. It can be like the municipality that goes into the city and records and then fixes the potholes, cuts back the weeds on the pathways and streets, and retrofits old buildings or tears down unnecessary structures. No one *out there* is hiding our hearts from us. The mirror of the heart, the city in the mirror, is everywhere and always reflecting. When we stop telling it what to reflect then the work begins.

We can get back to the heart, the pulsing center of the city in the mirror, the one emitting the reflections, but only after we stop using the heart as collateral. The city in the mirror, the tangled mess of our thoughts and desires, our projections and attachments, can be hard to live with. We try to buffer our hearts in many ways. One of my teachers, Sravana Borkataky-Varma, warns that we are too often "transactional." This is one of the most painful habits we carry. Once we get wise to the game, we can stop playing it. We can stop bartering the heart.

Bartering the Heart

The mind is transactional, and it uses its own peace—the heart—as currency. The mind says to life, "Let me pay you in heart currency, and I will get what I want."

Living with a transactional mind is painful because it creates and then it justifies suffering and unhappiness. This is how we keep our hearts closed and stop our process from even beginning, how we stay enthralled by the city in the mirror, while we're just swirling in the coil of hidden agreements.

The young queen, Snow White's stepmother, was so lost in compulsion that she could only hear back, "You are the fairest of them all." This made her happy. She believed her happiness rested only on her beauty. She believed, "I will be happy if I am the fairest." Her happiness required a daily check in: "Am I still the fairest?" She was willing to barter her happiness day after day on this same question. This is compulsion.

The Goddess path, step one, is reducing or eliminating all transactional thinking. We cannot get any further in our Goddess path if we do not stop bartering our own hearts. Understanding this step is essential before we can map anything else. Here is what this looks like: Transactional thinking always starts when the mind makes an exchange, starting with the hidden phrase, "I will be happy when…"

Classic ways we engage in transactional thinking with our deep inner truth might look like one of the following statements.

"I will be happier when my job is better, and I'm making more money."

"I would be happier if I had a different boss."

"I will finally find peace when I find the right partner. When I fall in love, that person will complete me."

"I am dissatisfied with my body weight and will find joy and acceptance when I hit my goals and my body looks different."

"I will be happy when my partner starts doing therapy."

"If my child gets into the right school or receives that honor, then I will finally be at peace."

"If I had not suffered that terrible loss, then I could be peaceful now."

"I would be happy if I were enlightened."

"Spiritual masters seem happy. I will be happy if I become a spiritual master, too."

"I would feel more love if my partner acknowledged me or at least tried to listen."

Please think for a moment, and then fill in your own statement here. If you have more than one agreement then start with the loudest or most current: *I will be happy when. I will find peace when…*

Most of the time, we do not know that these words are embedded in the full sentence of our thoughts. Instead, our thoughts are a clipped version of the whole sentence, something like "I should lose weight" or "I need to find a life partner."

Any time we have a *should* or a *need to* or a *if only* we can be close to certain that there is a full sentence making use of bartering the heart tucked in there. The "should" easily stops the complete thought, the part of the sentence that says, "I will be happy when," which more honestly reveals the mechanism of our suffering. When we use half of the sentence it's like we're looking at the city in the mirror and we're saying, "Only this road leads to the temple." Of course, all paths lead to all places, but the reflection can be very convincing.

Reestablishing reverence in the heart means taking this first step. It means applying our curiosity to these hidden statements. Listen to the whole sentence. You might be surprised at what you hear. When we complete the sentence, so to speak, we see that what we are doing is trying to bargain with life. If we can practice finishing the sentence, then we will at least be able to see what we're saying to ourselves.

This is why we start by writing out the full sentence. If we do not write out the full sentence then we may not see the agreement we are bartering in our heart. It's just as honest for the mind to say to itself, *I will be happy when I make more money,* as when it states, *I should get a better job.* If anything, being honest with the full sentence gives us a lot more to work with because, while we're still making an agreement, at least we can see what we're up to. This opens the door to curiosity. We delay our happiness and peace in the present because we think we only deserve that happiness and peace once we have hit our objective in the future.

Understand Your Bartering Statement

We are simply writing down our bartering statements. Your statement might be, "I'll be happy when my partner starts to see me, to pay attention, and to acknowledge me." This is where we need to pause. We need to feel what it feels like to carry our statements. We must feel what we feel. We must not jump into the dark and twisted avenues that lead out from these statements, trying to control, manage, or soothe our statements. We are looking in the mirror. We need to stand in front of this house, this garden, this street corner in the mirror, and stay for a bit.

There are a few ways that we might jump away from feeling our statement. We might try to let it go. We might try to justify. We might try to call the statement wrong or crazy. I am not implying that your statement is wrong or incorrect. I am only inviting you to pay attention to your bargaining statement. In the above example, I am not implying your partner does not need to go to therapy. We don't know that. We only know that your heart has made a bargain and that it has given away its happiness for something that is *not*.

Kick the Log and the River Will Flow

It is important to take a moment here to clarify that when we ask ourselves these questions and when we listen to the whole sentence of our inner bargaining, we are engaging agency within our hearts. If we are in an abusive or unsupportive environment then we may in fact discover that removing ourselves from that environment is what our heart needs. Psychiatrist Milton Erickson famously said, "If you kick the log, the river will start flowing." If your partner needs support, you can pursue that. If you need to make more money to support your family, then figure out a way to do that.

These solutions must unfold slowly and with curiosity. It's possible that we have held ourselves in very uncomfortable, dangerous, or unhealthy circumstances precisely because we have not ever asked ourselves where we are bartering our hearts. This is serious stuff and the implications can be life-changing.

When we stop bargaining with the future, we may discover that there is no hope of happiness in the present moment. If that's the case, we can address it—slowly, and with reverence. This may be the only honest way to address our needs in the present moment: without the fog of *maybes* and *shoulds* and *could-bes* clouding our hearts. Ramana Maharshi said, "Wanting to reform the world without discovering one's true Self is like trying to cover the world with leather to avoid the pain of walking on stones and thorns. It is much simpler to wear shoes. Happiness is your nature. It is not wrong to desire it. What is wrong is seeking it outside when it is inside." When we start to address our inner transactions, we can once again access our happiness.

I was once describing a health condition to a friend, something that flares up in me periodically and that creates a lot of suffering in my body and in my mind. I said to her at that moment, "I feel like I'm broken. I feel like I'm losing hope. I feel like if I can't fix this then I can't be happy." What I began to understand is that I had lost my ability to wobble like the raindrop because I was in pain. I had become rigid. Like the raindrop that collects around the dust particle, I needed to bring back my wobble. But because I was in constant distress, I had become more and more stiff: "I will be happy when I fix this."

Remember that resilience is the ability to fall in all directions and come back to center. The raindrop can wobble in all directions, but it always comes back to center. When we get rigid then things get dangerous. The bouncier a thing is the more it can fall this way or that way and know where to return. When something needs help and that rigidity starts to form then our system is telling us something. It's saying, *pay attention*.

I found that staying curious allowed me to keep living, not day by day, but second by second, holding joy and pain at the same time. I stopped bypassing my experiences. My mirror did not say, "You are the fairest of them all." It did not even say, "Hey girl, you're doing alright." My mirror said, "Clear out the day—this is going to be a bad one! And P.S., you are failing at life!" But because I have cultivated curiosity, I was able to bring it way down. Moment to moment. Here is the fear. Here is the despair.

The more curious I get, the more I'm able to wobble. I try new things. I'm deeply imperfect and I go back to bargaining every once in a while, but now I can say, "Oh! I'm bargaining my heart! It's not worth it to me to do that." Once I stop bargaining with my body, saying to it, "I'll be happy once you get fixed," then I can actually live. I might cry, and that's ok. I pray. A lot. I meditate. I sit in the trouble. I remember the Goddess. I remember that Mother Earth hurts, too. I remember my humanity, as well as all of the animals and the plants. I remember the tides. The point is that curiosity can keep me engaged and it can stop my process from calcifying, from getting rigid. Remember, when curiosity goes away it is a sign that things have gotten very rigid and closed down.

Completing the sentence makes our actions clearer because we may finally see what we are trying to communicate to ourselves. We may even stop purposely punishing ourselves in this present moment and delaying our happiness based on a transactional thought. We may strive for more support where it's needed and also accept wholeness and joy in this moment when that shows up, surprised and refreshing, at our heart's door. We need not barter away our present peace for a future version of ourselves, real or unreal.

Transactions Feed Transactions

More often than not, when we get to that goal: say it's the ideal weight, or we land that new job, or we find that partner that we have wanted for so long, we realize that we are still dissatisfied. A new transaction appears. Unhappiness followed us to our goal. Our solution is often to pick up and make a new bargain, and the cycle continues. We simply switch from one bargaining statement to another.

So when we stop operating on hidden agreements, we may have the information and the answers to make real choices. Sometimes we can make clear choices internally. But it's also possible that saying yes to the heart may mean standing up for our well-being or for a loved one or making a choice where we need to make a shift in our lifestyle.

Taking away transactional thinking can have profound effects. Investigation does not lead to passivity in our lives: the heart is luminous, silent, and powerful. When it becomes an active partner in our lives, when we have direct access at all times to the mirror of life inside of our being, the reflections start to change. Be open to what your heart is saying and the rest will unfold. It may tell you to change something in the real world.

Let's go back to your original statement: *I will be happy when...* Write it out one more time, right where you are at this moment. Can you bring some wobble to it? Can you be curious with your bargaining statement? When curiosity comes in, does the statement change? Is it really something else altogether? Did it start in one place and end up in another? What does it look like now?

If we believe that there is something for us to gain, some more perfect version of ourselves waiting around the corner, then we will forever be trapped in hope, anticipation, worry, and anxiety. These are the core aspects of clinging thought upon which our suffering grows and blossoms. Transactional thinking needs fuel to perpetuate itself. These forms of mind-created desire are how we barter away our awareness in this present moment and give up our peace.

As transactional thinking, desire always takes us away from being present with ourselves. When we get curious and explore desire, we find two broad categories of desire (or attachment). One form of desire is deeply unhelpful and it tends to drive the vast majority of our thoughts and emotions, particularly the reactive ones. It is where suffering is birthed. Almost all forms of thought-driven suffering fall into one of the four subcategories of this kind of desire.

The other form of desire is small and particular to the Goddess path, but because it is provisionally helpful to us, it deserves to be named and appreciated. We will get to the helpful form of desire, too, but we must first address the less helpful kind.

Desire that Doesn't Help

The types of desire that do not help us in our self-inquiry practices are always time-based, goal-oriented, and constructed of fixed thought patterns, binding us in the scaffolding of fear, lack, craving, and pain. Desire has four forms: two that look forward in time to the future and two that look backward in time to the past.

For each projection outside of the present moment and into the future or past, there is a positive and a negative desire polarity. There is a positive and negative future desire and a positive and negative past desire. This is the same desire, but we use different words to describe it, so we don't often see that the energy is the same vibration radiating outward, saying "I will be happy when," toward the future positive and negative, and the past positive and negative.

1. Hope and anticipation

Forward-looking, positive desire is called hope or anticipation. It is the term most closely associated with the common use of the word *desire*. It is when we desire an outcome and believe that this outcome will make us better or more whole. Transactional thinking falls into this category. When we hope for more money, a better job, a happier relationship, more ease with our parents or children, for the world to change, or that politics line up more closely with what we think is "right," then we are pushing our current pain into the future with a futile hope that out there somewhere in time we will get better or find a solution or be more complete.

When I was a young woman, I thought I would be happier if I lost weight, stayed very thin, and looked a certain way. I outgrew this thinking by doing deep and profound work on falling in love with myself and my body, just as it is. Then I encountered this body image problem again as a parent when my own daughter was young. She all of a sudden stopped wanting to go to the beach. We had loved going to the beach and this sudden resistance, which included tears, was very confusing. After some prompting, she finally said, "I don't want to put on a bathing suit because my legs are fat."

I was shocked. Our family does not use words like "fat" and I didn't know where she had heard the word nor how this had become hooked in her mind. I couldn't get to the bottom of the story until I realized that I didn't need to. I simply sat with her and completed the sentence. I said, "I think I hear what you're saying. If you're saying 'my legs are fat and so I'm unlovable' and you think that you can't be loved by me or Daddy, then I want you to know that it's not true. No matter what you look like, no matter what shape your body is in, I will love you and Daddy will love you, exactly how you are." She looked at me and cried, and we hugged. It took a few more conversations saying this same thing, and then one day her fear vanished and she was perfectly ok to put on a bathing suit and go to the beach again.

You may be familiar with this feeling now if you find your own subtle thought agreement: *I will find peace when...* This is the exact mechanism by which we barter away our current peace in exchange for a theoretical peace that we believe will be discovered in the future. Another name for hope or anticipation is craving. We crave something powerfully, and this creates suffering. By pushing the resolution to our current agitation into the future, we engage in one of the most painful forms of attachment and desire that leads to the breakdown of those very jobs and relationships that are creating frustration in this moment.

2. Worry and anxiety

Forward-looking negative desire is called worry or anxiety. Doctors have long understood that the physiology of stress does physical, emotional, and mental damage to us and even contributes to our survival metrics. While it may seem strange to call worry and anxiety forms of desire, it becomes clear once we see that the desire is inexorably linked to the outcome or the cessation of the object of our anxiety.

In some ways we might even say that anxiety is the anticipation or excitability that some future outcome is resolved, passed, or dissolved. The body does not know the difference between excitement and agitation. We get the jitters in both states. Likewise, by deeply tuning into our anxiety we can see that we are full with a form, albeit an uncomfortable form, of excitement.

The anxiety of an intense phone conversation or work deadline really translates as: "I am excited for this terrible thing to pass. I can't wait for it to be resolved." If you ever have anxiety about showing up to a social event, you might really be thinking, *I'm excited for this event to be done so that I can come back home, put on my comfortable clothing, rest by myself, with no one to impress or talk to or share small chat with.* And if we follow our full sentence, it might be: *I will be happy when this social event is over so I can go back to being comfortable and quiet in my own space, wearing my pajamas, where I don't have anyone to impress.*

Anxiety is not only social. It is deeply connected to our trauma patterns, the physical body, and even spiritual crisis. Almost all forms of separation from the infinite are a kind of anxiety, and so anxiety is what comes through when we feel isolated, separated, or in spiritual conflict.

3. Nostalgia and rose washing

Backward-looking desire that is positive is called nostalgia. This is when we idealize and rose-wash past states, thoughts, events, and relationship agreements because we wish to return to those times. We believe that we left our happiness behind and that if we can recreate those circumstances, we will again feel whole in this moment. We are bartering our peace and happiness with the past and giving our power to our imagination and memory, often in a way that doesn't reflect the truth of the past so much as a selected and amplified cross-section of past associations. This is when we believe things were better *then*, more complete *then*, and *if only we could return*, we would be happy.

Some people recall high school or their time in university as the best time of their lives. They've conveniently forgotten the stress of break-ups, scholastic failures, being rejected by that love interest, major exams, family unrest, social drama, and all of the complexity of living life, and only remember a feeling of having fun or being accepted or having less responsibility. Any time someone says to their partner or friend, "Why can't you be the person I used to know?" they are expressing a painful form of desire tied into a transactional thought that includes rose-washing.

If the present moment is full of pain and agony, then nostalgia only fuels the agony by keeping us attached to memories—some true and some partially truthful or even totally false—that do not have the power to resolve the pain of the current moment.

4. Shame and if-onlys

Backward-looking negative desire is called shame or regret, and it is almost always associated with trauma or negative memory. Trauma itself is not a form of attachment, but rather, a type of experience. But some ways we interact with our experiences, especially the shaming and regretting patterns, are a form of painful attachment.

Desire is how we bargain with the experience of trauma and turn that experience into shame. This is when we wish we had known better back then than we do now. This is when we apply our current perspective retroactively. This is when we willingly wound ourselves deeper by blaming ourselves for not knowing in the past what we believe we know now. I can think of no thought that holds more suffering than, *I wish it had been different and if only I had known*. I have a friend who was married to a narcissist, and for years she would shame herself by saying, "I wish I had seen it! The signs were so obvious. Now I know exactly what narcissism looks like, and just imagine how much happier I would be now if I had known then. I can't believe I let myself be abused like that." This translates as, "I would be at peace now if I had never experienced the pain of living with a narcissistic partner."

The desire here is to have a different past, to be a better person within our own purview when we investigate our memories and actions, and to project our current state of process on our previous states of process. Shame is one of the most painful forms of desire we cycle because we compound the pain that we already feel connected to those events with our deep judgments.

We also add blame and we direct that blame in real-time toward those events. We magnify the original wound by shame, making it more real and dramatic by this force. We make the wound more permanent by bringing shame into trauma. The trauma happened, but instead of working with that directly, we apply shame onto the wound and barter away any agency over our process. When we start to see that we are bargaining our present heart with a past experience we can begin to gain back that agency within ourselves by recognizing our wholeness.

When my friend started to reclaim her bargaining statements, she stopped blaming her ex as much and started saying things like, "I'm noticing this new manager at work is a narcissist. I can see the pattern now. It's very clear to me and I recognize it right away. I was able to stand up for myself in that work situation yesterday because I could see the situation clearly. It felt good to stand up for myself."

There is a form of this past-negative desire that is spiritual in nature: resolving karma. Some people feel that the spiritual path has a lot to do with cleaning up past life traumas. This is the same mechanism as this particular desire but with fancier words and a fancier purpose. *I will find peace when my karma is seen and resolved.*

Just think–whole cultures have kept oppressive social structures going for thousands of years by saying, "Well, the reason you're so poor and have a terrible life is that you were a bad person in a previous life. You are just paying the price for that bad karma now, and there is nothing you can do about it. You can't help it and you have to live with that. Your poverty is your own business, and the best thing you can do about it is try to improve your karma this time around so that you can come back in the next life with more success." This very problematic and abusive justification is only possible when operating on this particular form of shame-attachment. I do happen to believe that past-life patterns are some of the traumas and activations that we face in the current time. But again, when we get curious, the stories that unfold or that are seen do not need to be bargained with. Patterns are simply seen. Once a pattern is seen and digested it loses its power.

I have a handy tool in my kitchen that can grab a tight jar lid and help it to open. Curiosity is like that. When something is tightly wound up and keeps the jar locked up then we need help opening the lid. Seeing our patterns, whether they come from this life or from other more mysterious places, whether they are karmic or energetic or universal, is more about being able to open the jar lid and look inside. The Goddess loves to look inside. There is nothing like opening the jar lid and taking a good look inside the jar. This takes the pain out of our shame and our if-onlys.

Desire that Helps

For many there is a deep driving force that propels us on the spiritual path of self-inquiry. This positive desire centers on wanting to wake up from the thoughts and patterns that hold us in suffering; wanting to abide in peace without having that peace contingent upon circumstances, memories, or projections. This is the desire to achieve spiritual peace and the ability to come home to the heart in all places and at all times. Nisargadatta Maharaj calls this "earnestness," the one helpful form of desire. It is an eager and available dedication to our own unfolding. This quality keeps us practicing the things that help us, whether it is meditation, or walking without distraction, or taking small pauses throughout the day to check in with our hearts, or joining a community of like-minded seekers.

Earnestness is another word for curiosity, though it is perhaps more organized and committed to that central desire of awakening to the heart. We may not be there yet. Some layers might be hidden. We may be carrying more patriarchal patterns in our hearts than we know. We may not know how to linger in the heart. We may have glimpsed moments of the heart or moments of total silence but are not yet established in that wisdom. Earnestness is what we use to track the inner progress of our curiosity and steer it deeper into our experiences.

Earnestness means that we are willing to stumble through the deeper layers of ourselves no matter what we learn today, tomorrow, and next week. We know we will keep going. It means we are available and committed to awakening our curiosity. Like the proverbial finger that points to the moon, it is the type of desire that directs us to look at luminosity. It is the finger that points. It cannot take us all the way there, for awake curiosity is independent, free, and already complete within our hearts, but when our eyes follow that path, we know our intention more clearly.

When we begin to clean up our desire attachments and begin to reveal the heart, we realize that the heart is perfectly capable of interacting with flexibility, resilience, and clarity because it is responding from the present moment. Acting from the heart center means being able to access a space inside of ourselves that is big—big enough to hold the complex and the difficult, the hard and the beautiful. This is a worthy place to live from and it always allows our experiences, those reflections in the mirror, to dynamically shine outward and return back into the heart core.

▼ ▼ ▼

A Practice

Notice what you notice.

1. **Breathe.** Follow your breath in order to shine your curiosity into your body.
2. **Identify a Transactional Thought.** Write down some of the goals that you carry in your heart. These might be subtle goals that take a while to identify or they might be explicit goals that you have written down in the past. Some goals that are common might be:
    - Success in my profession.
    - A healthy relationship with my parents, with my children, with my partner.
    - Love.
    - More financial stability.
    - Spiritual success, recognition of my heart, or enlightenment.
3. **Finish the Sentence.** In front of the goal that you have written down, write the words: "I will find peace when" or "I will be happy when," and feel into this more complete sentence. See if this complete sentence has tendrils that stretch into other aspects of your life. How big is your agreement? How big is your transaction?
4. **Hold Yourself in Awake Curiosity.** Ask yourself: Where am I bartering away my inner peace in this moment to achieve peace, in the form of my goal, in the future? Can I experience peace now

without reserving it for the future? Notice where this thought lives in thought, emotion, or in your body.

5. **Reclaim Your Body.** Spend a moment to bring in all of your energy, all of your own life force. Have you given away some of your energy to other people or to a project or to a space? Recall that energy back into your body. Then see if you have collected any energy that does not belong to you—gathered from someone else or someone else's space. Let that energy flow back to that person and out of your body. Feel what it is like to have sovereignty of your own physical and energetic body.
6. **Notice a Breath.** Breathe in the sovereignty of your own energy, complete and whole. Breathe as long as you need to, until you feel and enjoy the wholeness.

CHAPTER 4

Layers of Being

WHEN WE GET very quiet, we can feel the rise and fall of our chest. We can hear our own soft breath. When we need a deep rest, we often turn toward the rhythm of soothing music or the sounds of nature. Surfers might spend hours sitting on the giant body of the ocean. We rock our children when they are sad or tired. We rock our bodies in deep meditation. We sleep well by the river or in a gentle rain. We often think that we need to stop and be still when we are exhausted. But what if, in our need for deep rest, we are not looking for that total stillness itself but are instead looking to get quiet enough to sense the vibrations all around us?

Once the mirror of the heart is uncovered we begin to understand that this mirror, the deep reflective heart, is not some still surface, disconnected from the content and the stories that are reflected. They are interactive, interwoven, and inseparable. They dance in rhythm. The heart has a heartbeat.

When I bring up the heart you might ask, "what do you mean by *the heart*?" We refer to the heart in many ways: as the physical organ of the heart that moderates blood through our bodies; as the poetic heart that holds our emotional center that we often refer to when we have big feelings; as our wisdom and intuition center; or even the point of total stillness that we turn to inside of ourselves to find deep and abiding quiet.

To all of these I say, “yes. *The heart is that.*”

The heart has layers and each layer must be seen. I refer to the heart that expresses and includes all of the layers, claiming each with flexible totality. Because the heart is vast, we need help navigating the layers so that we can emerge with a complete understanding of our wholeness.

We have a physical heart that contains the heartbeat, the embodied experience, and the material world which expands and contracts.

We have an emotional-thinking layer in the heart.

We have an intuitive layer.

We have, too, the transcendent dissolve of absolute stillness.

And finally, we have the total reflective whole, the dynamic and pulsating silence that I call curiosity, playing the scales up and down these other four layers. All of the layers have rhythm and they have direction. This rhythm, the expansion and contraction, is what we call vibration. We might call this vibration *sound* or *the Word*. The Word as creation, you likely know, is not a new concept.

Rhythm and Pulse

In the Bible, Genesis begins: “Then God said, ‘let there be light,’ and there was light,” revealing the Word of God as the first vibration of existence out of the void and darkness. God spoke before he created and as the means to create. In many ways his power lies in his ability to command. The origin of creation in this system signals forth through *sound:* “God said.” From sound emerges light.

Sound has long been represented by the Goddess. The earliest goddesses are often in charge of sound in some form: music, wisdom, scholarship, or rhythm. Sound is held by the Muses in Greek mythology, where Calliope is foremost.

My favorite goddess of sound, however, also happens to originally be a cow. Her name is Vāc. The Goddess Vāc represents sound in a woven myriad of Indian traditions. She is very old. In the Ṛg

Veda (1500 BCE), Vāc is the Goddess of the speech that empowers sacrifice and the cosmos. She proclaims: "Hear, one and all, the truth as I declare it...I breathe forth like the wind giving form to all created worlds; beyond the heaven, beyond this earth am I, so vast am I in greatness."[6]

The Abrahamic God in his seminal creation role issues forth light. But as sound, just before the creation of the light-dark polarity, as the vibration before the split, he was a *she*. She was the vibrating Word. We still honor her today through some of the most powerful words of daily life. Vāc is cognate with the Latin words *vox*, to speak, and *vocare*, to call. In English she spills into words like vocal, voice, vowel, advocate, invoke, evoke, and many others.

Mother Is the Sound in Your Heart

Two thousand years later the Goddess Mātṛkā, a form of Vāc, is described in certain tantras as the source and expression of all vibration that lies coiled in the heart. This coil or knot pours forth from the heart through the alphabet into form. The term Mātṛkā (pronounced *mah-trih-kaah*) means, among other things, *Mother*. The alphabet is the *matrix*. These two words, mother and matrix, are cognate with this all-embracing Goddess Mātṛkā. The mother, the matrix, and the alphabet that produces and enrobes matter (do you hear it again?) are one and the same.

This mother-matrix vibrates outward from the heart, rippling into being through layers of pulsation that range from total silence, or precognitive sound, through intention, emotion, and thought, to the hollering of the baby and the intergalactic universe. A great medieval sage writes:

> The knowing subject has as its essence the supremely subtle vibration of the Self. Its nature is one of contraction and expansion, that is, opening and closing. The more this combination of expansion and

> contraction becomes evident in the vibration of the Heart, of the triangle, etc., the more does the subjectivity become elevated.... Conversely, the more the expansion and contraction diminish, the more does the subjectivity fall until it becomes inert like a stone.[7]

The main difference between the big bang theory and the cosmogenesis that Vāc and those traditions that celebrate pulsation represents is in the observation by the latter that creation did not happen *out there* in the strange and magnificent "separate" universe, creating our sentience as some fantastic and unexplainable byproduct of energy and matter as they spill out and then condense again, but happens constantly and continuously *in here*, in the center of your heart and my heart and The Heart, always creating itself, hovering for a moment, dissolving itself, forgetting itself, and remembering itself.

The big bang is consciousness and consciousness pulsates. The big bang, at least the tantric one, is consciousness *as sound vibration*. The big bang describes sentience itself, which breathes. The point of creation in the heart is like the tight coil of all matter and energy, like the tiny seed that holds the map of the huge tree. It is the sprout. It is the matrix of sound yet to be expressed, or the center of gravity that swallows and spits, condenses and creates. In other words, the Goddess is calling us through our hearts using sound vibration which, like a drop of water that falls into a very still lake, ripples outward in a series of concentric circles. She is calling the liquid of our very being directly and boldly.

She is remarkably well-organized while she creates and reabsorbs. The Goddess path, after all, is a map, and it's a map that can be described and then walked. The heart's layers have a sequence to them, just as the ripples in the pond can be seen and described, layer by layer.

The Map of the Heart

The heart is the Word, described with exactitude through the Goddess of Sound and Creation.[8] The heart has several nested layers that operate upon one another, each acting as a holographic reality where that layer contains the pattern of the whole. All of the layers share the core traits of heartbeat: of expansion and contraction, systole and diastole, creation and destruction, emission and absorption, contained and expressed in its rhythmic beat that we know so well.

The heartbeat is life, not only for the body, but for all of consciousness. The layers that we experience start with the physical heart that can be seen and measured in the body. It can be touched, monitored, and watched as it expands and contracts, interacting closely with the lungs and circulatory system in a deep electric rhythm that sets the foundation for life, circulation, and exchange of elements, nutrients, and information in the body.

Every layer of the heart must be seen as equal in beauty and holiness. It is useful to see what it looks like to get stuck on any one layer of the heart, to prioritize a layer, or to fetishize it. This analysis covers almost all of human psychology, especially spiritual psychology, and gives us a simple model to see where we have understood or misunderstood our inner journey.

The physical layer

The physical layer of the heart is what we can touch with our senses—what we feel when we bring our hands to our skin, what we hear when we close our eyes under water and listen to the pulse. Because this layer interacts with the physical outside world, with the stuff and the noise out there, we can also say the outside world is an extension of or in direct contact with this layer.

The outside world, that which is not directly part of the body, is a part of the heart mirror. When it comes to the actual heart, we are starting in this model with the physical body and the organ that can be touched and that radiates out, through blood flow and fluids and venous return, into every single part of the human form.

It is what we find when we look—when we use our senses. When we take deep breaths through the nose and stay with that practice, we will eventually notice that the sound of the breath does not originate in the nostrils. Nor does the sound originate in the throat, as is often taught in breathing classes. If we stay with the breath, we will notice that the sound of the breath comes from the chest. The breath beat and the heart beat are interconnected.

The lungs and the heart are one system comprised of several organs that require one another to function. When we inhale, we expand the lungs, contracting the breathing muscles that push into the belly, and squeezing blood flow through and around the organs. When we exhale there is a depressurization of the organs as they are lightly dragged upward. Breathing returns passive blood from the veins back to the heart. It is one of the body's ways of bringing blood home to be cleaned and oxygenated at the heart.

Learning to slow down the breath and bring it all the way to the lungs is a beautiful practice. In tantra the breath is called the "ceaseless prayer," or the *ajapa japa*. A *japa* is a recitation, utterance, or the muttering of a sound. When the "a" is placed before a word in Sanskrit it means "not-that." So the *ajapa japa* is a way of saying *the silent utterance, the stillness that is sound, the unvoiced resonance*. It comes in and it goes out. As long as we are living, the breath comes in and it goes out. It works with the physical heart to expand, contract, squeeze and compress, decompress and circulate. The lungs and the heart unite. The heartbeat is the blueprint. The breath follows the blueprint. The whole body pulsates and radiates from that blueprint.

If we get stuck on the layer of the physical heart then we tend to be spiritually atheistic. We believe that the body and that the health of the body is of primary importance. We believe in science, what can be touched and observed, seen and handled, monitored and subjected to a hypothesis, along with a means of testing the hypothesis. We believe in the "matter model" of existence, where matter is all that exists, consciousness is produced by matter at some mysterious point after the creation of the universe, and western science has things all mapped out. Body, physical health, and western medicine are our temples.

The thought-emotion layer

The energetic or sensation layer of the heart is sometimes referred to as our emotional center, and includes the physical response in the chest to our feelings or exchanges with others. Our thoughts and emotions open and close.

When we see something extraordinarily beautiful our chest can feel so free and light, we feel as though our hearts could explode with joy; when someone says something cruel to us, we might feel a physical pain, tightening, or squeezing in our heart, and we might even lose our breath or clutch our breast; when we are especially excited or nervous, we can feel our heart shimmer between the two: "Look at that bright pink in the sunrise! It's so beautiful. Oh, but does that mean it will rain? If it rains, will it ruin my friend's birthday party? I hope she won't be crushed."

When we are scared, we might feel a kind of shallow skipping on the inside. These are things that can be felt deeply in the physical body but that cannot be measured by instruments beyond simply recording brain waves and heartbeat after they have already responded to the emotion. The origin of emotion cannot be touched by science. Our emotional rhythm has a heartbeat.

Our family members are great teachers of this emotional heartbeat. Sometimes my children come home from school devastated by something unkind someone said to them, bowing their heads and curling their shoulders into their chests. They will talk about how they feel it in their body. They might cross their arms over their chest in frustration or defiance.

When I tell my children I love how hard they are working on a project or look into their eyes and say, "Thank you for being so helpful," I can see them shine a little bit bigger. Their chest might swell a bit.

My own mother, at the age of eighty, also responds and closes down when she thinks someone is saying something critical to her. I also see her open brightly when her heart feels seen, or when someone is really interested in what she's saying. When my friend got roped into learning Italian with my mom she exclaimed to me, "It made her so happy! I think she grew an inch!" We swell when we are excited. At all ages and all walks of life our emotions open and close like the heartbeat.

When people refer to "my heart" in poetic terms they often refer to this layer, describing the heart that can be broken or joyful or sensitive or scared. This layer also includes our thoughts, emotions, and perceptions, and in this layer the emotional heart that craves love, happiness, and self-worth are expressed in various ways—each with a pulsation that moves outward or draws inward. Thoughts are part of this layer because thoughts and emotions are profoundly related such that they cannot be separated in the body.

With regards to the breath, this is the place where we experience the expansion and the contraction of our breathing as a monitor of our psychological state, and the place where we feel deep wounds and great joys reflected in breath. When we are emotional, we need only check our breath to reveal what this layer is communicating: the breath may be shallow and tight, shaky and constricted when we feel attacked or sad.

Our breath might be free and we might sigh loudly when we look upon a sunset or when we get out of a car after a long journey and feel our legs stretching toward the earth. Those sighs are potent. On the subtle level the heart may be protected or shielded through thick layers of pattern, thought, avoidance, or neglect.

We all know the sensation when our feelings are open or closed and we either want to reach out or pull back. If we do *not* know this sensation then we have created armoring around our hearts that is so thick that we have desensitized ourselves to the world. Spiritual practice, therapy, and deep compassion are necessary to address this numbing, which creates despair within ourselves and enacts all of the violence on earth.

If we get stuck on the thought-emotion layer of the heart, we tend to think of everything through the lens of psychology: how we feel, how we process, and how we think. If we are religious, then we are probably engaged in quieting or suppressing or dissolving this layer of the heart because it is where human emotion tugs and drags us and where the chatter of thoughts, true and untrue, tug at us and spin us in an endless wash. This is where Buddhism, especially Dzogchen, and classical or Patañjalian yoga do some of the most ingenious and helpful investigation into human nature.

Transactional thinking, bartering the heart, happens most frequently at this layer. After taking care of our physical health, addressing transactional thinking is the first step on the spiritual path of the heart because seeing this mechanism gets us through the gate of the heart and into the deeper layers. If we cannot get through our bartering then we cannot unlock the inner heart. Psychology, mental health, and the notion that "emotion creates reality" are our temples.

The intuitive-energetic layer

Just below, though part of, the sensing and emotional layer of the heart lies the intuitive layer—that quiet whisper of guidance that gives us truth, direction, and warning. Intuition is different from thought because it does not loop in repetitive circles nor does it reflect in activation patterns, but rather comes clear, quiet, unwavering, and unannounced.

It is not concerned with whether we listen to it or not, though we often suffer when we do not listen. Whereas the mind really, really cares if we pay attention to it, our intuition does not mind at all whether we hear it, ignore it, catch it, or miss it.

In sacred scripture from India, our deep intuition is described as the knowing that a bird has in choosing where to build her nest. In ancient Egypt, the word *Mother* was represented by a single glyph: a vulture. The Mother was symbolized by the vulture because the vulture has a deep instinct, almost a magical ability, to know where to find food, sustenance, and protection from far away distances.

The vulture appears deeply instinctive. Nature, especially as the winged creature, is full of intuition and deep inner communications that are quiet, certain, and fleeting. The vulture appears far before the Egyptian writing system and is part of a wider and more ancient Goddess worship around birds, particularly raptors and vultures, which symbolized life, death, and the communication between people and spirit to earlier peoples. The pulsation at the intuitive layer is steady, quiet, and requires deep listening, but its rhythm is unmistakable. The life force lives on this layer. Breath touches this space in profound ways.

Oftentimes when we experience trauma at the level of our intuition it is twofold. When we hear the whisper of the heart and we ignore that whisper then we feel the pain of what unfolds as a trauma. But we also experience the deeper, more lasting trauma of having abandoned our inner wisdom, that deeper pain of knowing that we did not listen. Of all the traumas that we experience, this deeper trauma is the hardest to reconcile for most people.

Intuition is a gift and it cannot be directly touched or seen. It comes to us in a dream or a subtle turn of the hand on the wheel of the car or a tug to move in a certain direction professionally or personally. Intuition comes unbidden and may or may not come when bidden. It comes through what some people call manifestation or deep remembering or synchronicity. Seeing a subtle pattern in the world around us clearly is a gift that we all have and it requires us to stay open, curious, and available to listen to the soft wings of our innermost knowing. In order to get this quiet, we must have moved with some success through the psychology of thought and emotion. We must have the tools to know the difference between thought and intuition.

Like the body layer and the thought-emotion layer of the heart, the breath is important in the energy layer. However, breath moves energy at this layer in very subtle ways. Eventually the breath mechanism itself is less important than the flow of energy that is so often (and nearly always in regular life) connected to breath. It's like breath, that is, *breathing*. The vehicle and the energy called *breath* is the passenger in the vehicle. At this layer of the heart the vehicle is important because it drives the passenger around, but it's also possible at this layer for the passenger to move freely outside of the vehicle. The act of breathing is not in charge here, but the movement of subtle breath, independent of the mechanism of the lungs, is queen. This subtle breath is called different things in different traditions, but most frequently is referred to as prana or chi/qi. There are whole practices in most esoteric systems, including tantra, where the breathing mechanics can stop entirely- the vehicle can park- and yet the energy still flows and moves in the deep body and heart. In these cases, the body does not die, even though the individual has stopped inspiration and expiration. Prana remains in circulation.

This layer is the home of the mystic. The wise woman. The priestess. The shaman and the psychic. Anyone who can read another person's history or deep patterning is listening to this layer. While this layer is always present, learning to listen to it is a skill that can be developed to some degree of more or less precision. This skill can be passed through a family line, say from mother to daughter or granddaughter, or from father to son or nephew. The way to develop this layer is not to *add* practices but to get out of our own way- to take away the noise that usually covers up our delicate wisdom antennae.

Prioritizing this layer of the heart means identifying as spiritual and seeing everything as energy. The occult and the New Age models are all about the deep impressions of the intuitive heart. Not the feelings generated by the mind, but the feelings that arise from the energy field. Slowing down is the lesson of this layer.

Living in California, I often see that this layer is what many people describe as spirituality. Many of the modern feminine arts, those related to sacred sex, witchcraft, and magic, can linger in or even stay trapped at this layer. Many of the shamanic practices and ceremonies, including the wildly popular world of psychedelics, address or gain access within this layer. From this layer the medicine can often connect to the other layers of the heart as well, becoming a ladder for us to explore the whole heart system.

This intuitive layer is also the domain of energy healing, "seeing things" about people or places, and understanding patterns that cannot be seen so easily. This often goes hand-in-hand with disbelieving the other models, like psychology or western medicine, that don't prioritize this space or that forget to include deep wisdom. If stuck at this layer we might hear someone say, "Don't go to the doctor—they never know anything. You need to heal your past life agreements and subtle energy systems through prayer and meditation." Depending on the place of injury, this might be good information, or it might be dangerous advice indeed.

When we are stuck at the intuitive layer of the heart, we might in fact become amazing healers, psychics, or intuitives. This is wonderful. However, without the integration of the physical and emotional parts of the heart we may be prone to bypass or even energetically injure those who stand before us.

My sister once went to a massage and the masseuse, whom she had never met, spent the hour bombarding her with unsolicited psychic information that left her in tears. These assaults of information happen rather commonly and it's a form of abuse, even though the one with the intuition may think it's good to share what they see—whether they have been given permission or not.

When taken out of balance, some of the worst spiritual gaslighting can happen at this layer because we may be able to dance between the magical and the void of transcendence that this layer rests upon, but we've not yet totally penetrated the void and then moved beyond the transcendent. Ironically, many people who are dancing this sword edge between intuition and transcendence posture or claim to be (even demand that they are) in the "beyond the transcendent" state, but the subtle energy of manipulation, of having an agenda, of communicating in any way that "I know better than you," belies the trap.

Transactional thinking happens rarely at this layer, since it really makes its home in the thought-emotion layer. However, some transactional thoughts that have to do with our spiritual growth and our awakening do refer to this deep energetic layer, and so seeing how we might barter our peace for a spiritual ideal may benefit from giving more agency, attention, and focus on this layer.

The transcendent layer

The deepest layer of the heart, the part that lives under the armoring of thoughts, emotions, perceptions, and just below intuition, is perfect silence. It is absolute listening and clear curiosity. It is the place from which our deepest consciousness arises and subsides. When we listen closely to the heart, we realize this stillness.

Every gap in our thoughts, in the active mind, is full of the heart. This stillness is not empty nor is it a vacuum, though it is often referred to as emptiness or the Void. It is dynamic but totally untethered to form. It is the radiance that creates, maintains, and destroys all experience, including thought and emotion, pain and pattern. More than that, it is the place that forgets its own self-awareness and remembers that same awareness. This gives the heart deep agency: the ability to remember itself and to forget itself in any moment is entirely free within its own accord. The silence at the heart somehow radiates a wild beauty. It knows itself. It births the whole universe.

As agency, its knowing of itself is what defines it: a kind of self-reflexivity and self-absorption that shimmers, shines, radiates, swells, and ripples away and then back again simultaneously. This fullness is the single feature of the heart core. The deep layer of the heart is the complete union of the movement and the silent impulses and energies within us, the collapse of all paired opposites into one whole. We can get stuck at this layer when we think that it's truer than the other layers. This is only possible when we have not completely seen beyond the transcendent, and are hanging out on the shores of the void. Getting stuck in the void happens when we adhere to the *transcendence bias* and *let it go* spirituality. This layer, as you have surely already observed, is the transcendent ideal of patriarchal religion and tradition. Taken in balance with the Goddess there is a wildly radical union and Aristotle's words: "The whole is greater than the sum of its parts," has no truer application.

At this layer, we have a choice of direction according to the depth of our recognition, Maha Samadhi (physical death), which is a completion of the divine masculine transcendent path, or Jivanmukti, the Goddess path, where embodied existence becomes a play of fullness at all of the layers of the heart.

The Saturation

There is a final integration of the heart called saturation, which is not exactly a layer, nor is it a single step deeper. We might call this state the beyond-the-transcendent. The beyond the transcendent is when we are equally present and totally integrated *on all of the layers* of the heart without preference for one layer over another in our lived experience. It is when we have accepted and integrated all of the previous four aspects of ourselves and stand to face our wholeness without needing to hold one layer above the rest.

Utpaladeva called this *cit*, or total integration of the divine with the immanent.

When we move beyond the transcendent, we have plumbed our absolute depths, without getting stuck on any layer of the heart. We are willing to touch each layer with reverence, frequently, and at will. Beyond the transcendent is embodiment of a deeper nature. I call it embodying the Goddess. It is what the Goddess path can reveal when we get very honest and very committed to our inner process. Beyond the transcendent is best described as living with awake curiosity.

By working our way through the layers of the heart, by recognizing or remembering our self-luminous sovereignty, we are slowly accepting and experiencing each stratum in order to shine at all levels of the heart's healthiest expression. There is a natural pulsation, a heartbeat, to this process in which we contract and expand and in which our experiences are reborn and absorbed back again. This process is part of the natural pulsation of being. The heartbeat is designed to bring us closer to the heart's still center, calling us homeward through rhythm and using that rhythm and pulse to mirror the activities of our perceptions, thoughts, and experiences upon our center.

When we give all of our heart layers agency, we may finally find the lasting antidote to *let it go* spirituality. "It's all emptiness." "None of this is real." "Find salvation." I'm not saying that these phrases and the philosophies that birth them are all wrong, but they are misleading. Or rather, they are incomplete without the embrace of curiosity, the embodied choreography of the Mother, the easy saturation of those statements without subordinating the other layers of our deep reflective being.

You are (if you are reading this) dynamically alive, full of complexity, and engaged in all kinds of relationships with all kinds of living and subtle beings, systems, and patterns. You have a body and a process-driven mind for a reason. The great Siddha teacher Swami Muktananda, himself influenced by the tantric teachings, once said to his students, "If you can't find it here, in the body, where are you going to find it?" He meant we must turn toward this form, this life, to understand the complex and seamless reality. We are called here to turn toward our relationships, our transactional agreements, our life experiences, and this living temple called the body. Put together, stillness and dynamic movement form the whole truth, which is a place that's shockingly joyful, alive, constantly changing, and utterly whole all at the same time.

The body matters, as Muktananda often said. The path of the Goddess through curiosity means using life, our bodies, our lived experience, our feelings, our needs, as a dynamic and self-luminous city in the mirror that shines at all times back to the heart through its many layers.

▼ ▼ ▼

A Practice

Place your hands on your heart. One over the other, or side by side. Feel your heartbeat. Feel that which expands and contacts. Notice the blueprint. Notice your center.

1. **Breathe.** Make your exhalation twice as long as your inhalation until you can inhale for four counts and exhale for eight. This stimulates the vagus nerve (in your brain stem) and helps to calm the nervous system. Shine your curiosity into your body.
2. **Notice Your Body.** Place a hand someplace that calls to you in your body: a pleasant and expansive sensation, a tight and constricted sensation, something hot or ragged. Something simply that calls to you. Contemplate that sensation totally. Turn toward it. Notice all the senses involved: is there a shape, a color, a heat, a texture, a direction? Without going into the story, just

feel the totality of the sensation. If a story is clearly tied into the sensation, then try to simply feel the sensation for several breaths or even a few minutes.

3. **Recall the Thought, Emotion, or Story.** If the body sensation eventually wants to reveal an emotion or story, then allow the body to do so. Try not to let the mind search for a story. Let the body unfold itself. If a story or emotion comes up, write it down. Take your journal and write from the lens of the body, not the mind. "I feel hot when," or, "The sharpness in my breath is telling me," etc. Keep the perspective from the body up to the emotions or thoughts.
4. **Make Use of Your Healing Community.** If you need an ally or professional to help you understand your material, then find that for yourself. Do the work. Uncover the whole story.
5. **Listen to Your Intuition.** You may notice that when you do strong work on the body and thought-emotion layers of the heart, your deep inner knowledge begins to pipe up. This is your intuition turning on. If intuition has something to say, then listen. Gather more information. Write it down. Come back to it once you know more.
6. **Get into Nature.** When we are exploring the body as an entry point into the heart, it is helpful to find a rock to sit on, a tree to look at, a river to make friends with. If you do not live close to nature then get a house plant and tend to it. Soil, healthy soil, soil without pesticides and chemicals, is so healthy for us. One study showed that putting our hands in soil for ten minutes a day, by gardening, by walking barefoot on clean earth, had strong antidepressant effects. A bacterium called *Mycobacterium vaccae* gets absorbed through contact, which activates serotonin receptors in the body. Being in nature is good for our physical and mental bodies.

CHAPTER 5

The Body Layer

THE HUMAN BODY is a miracle. The heart beats, the breath breathes in and out, the skin expands and contracts. Everything pulsates. The body has arches that build upon themselves to create a cathedral around the heart. The feet have arches that build into the ankles, knees, hip joints, pelvic basin of bones, and the diaphragm of the pelvic floor that allows our breath, as well as the diaphragms along the spine that billow out and back again to the heart. The chamber of the mouth is arched, the throat, the skull. The arches of the body are like one huge system of flying buttresses, continued from the widest reaches of the universe, supporting and drawing always back to the heart, the center of the cathedral.

There is a teaching story about the father that asks the child to bring him water. The child goes into the other room and comes back with a cup of water. The father says, "I asked you to bring me water, not a cup." Perplexed, the child goes back with the cup and returns with a bowl full of water. Again, the father says, "I asked you to bring me water, not a bowl." The child tries again with a plate, and the response returns the same. Finally, the child comes to the father with cupped hands full of leaking water, and the father says, "I asked you to bring me water, not hands. Do you see that water needs a vessel?

Water, like breath, life, and knowledge, need a vessel." The lesson is that the body matters. The body is the vessel that holds our water, our breath, our life, our knowledge, and our curiosity.

Please Breathe

A sign as large as a billboard that spreads across the lobby of the yoga studio where I have taught for nearly two decades reads, "Please Breathe." Breath is an unfolding of the pulsating universe. It also impacts nearly every aspect of the embodied experience. In the human body, the lungs and the heart function together to bring information and nutrients into circulation. Breath nourishes blood vessels and this saturated blood is then circulated and spun through the heart's helix-like tubes to move the blood into the body. Blood reaches out to the far corners of the body because the heart draws it there, and breath is one of the functions that brings blood back to the heart.

Breathing also impacts the nervous system and the trauma response in the body. The trauma and addiction researcher Dr. Gabor Maté teaches that trauma is not what happens to you, but is what happens inside you as a result of the event. Most people have experienced some trauma in their lives. Situations do not impact people uniformly. Dr. Bessel van der Kolk says in his seminal book, *The Body Keeps the Score*, "Stress is not an inherent property of events themselves. It is a function of how we label and react to them."[9] What might create trauma in one person may not create trauma, or stored body impressions, in another.

When trauma is released from the body it often does so through the breath. Physical release of tensions in the body or trauma by talking about or reliving the experiences that caused the trauma are called *abreactions*. When we relive our traumas, we often gasp, hold our breath, breath rapidly and shallowly, or even laugh. Notice how much the breath is involved in many of our trauma responses. Notice, too, how the body relies on pulsation (gasping, laughing, crying) to release trauma. Dr. van der Kolk goes on to say: "Our sense of agency, how much we feel in control, is defined by our relationship with our bodies and its rhythms: Our waking and sleeping and how we eat, sit, and walk define the contours of our days. In order to find our voice, we have to be *in* our bodies—able to breathe fully and able to access our inner sensations. This is the opposite of dissociation, of being 'out of body' and making yourself disappear."[10]

As a long-time yoga teacher, yoga therapist, and lead trainer in trauma-informed yoga trainings and workshops, I've seen hundreds of people experience abreactions by getting back into their bodies, their breath, agency, and curiosity, allowing them to release tensions and patterns that they may not have known were there. Many of the exercises of yoga movements and breathing help to balance the nervous system. Breathing with an exhale that is two times longer than the inhale and humming (as we do when we chant) helps the nervous system by countering stress, anxiety, and irritation. My body has responded to my own traumas and anxieties by crying, laughing, breathing quickly, breathing deeply, humming, and many other physical responses.

That breath is used in trauma work, therapy, and counseling is well researched and uncontroversial. Breath has also been used in other interesting or eyebrow raising ways. Some breathing practices, like Stanislav Grof's Holotropic Breathwork, are designed to induce psychedelic experiences, perhaps by mimicking forced abreactions. Other breathing practices have had a more religious and social application, like certain yogic *pranayamas* described in ancient Indian texts called *Puranas*. In them, breathing techniques were assigned prescriptively and proscriptively by orthodox Brahmins in the case these elevated men came across some intolerable pollution, such as accidentally interacting with someone of a low social caste. To them breathing was medication and purification.

Breath has a wide range indeed. It touches our deepest fears, traumas, safety, and claims to agency. The body and breath have been responding to our emotional states our whole lives.

In yoga, I heard (and taught) for decades that in the physical body it is important to "draw the shoulder blades down the back." When we draw our shoulder blades away from our ears, we counter some of the shrugging tension that plagues us and it helps our posture. The problem with this physical cue is that it stops us from breathing. I cannot understand why we still use this cue so frequently in movement modalities, other than my guess that it makes the shape look better. Maybe it's time to reevaluate.

In order to take a full and complete breath, the top three ribs, which lift out to the sides and up toward the armpits like water spigot handles, need to move. Try it now. If you can slightly lift the head of your arm bones and deepen your armpits (I often say, "Free your armpits!"), you might notice that your top ribs have more movement. When the top three ribs move, the highest and first in the chain, the rest of the ribs can follow. You can also try my breathing exercise in this chapter for a technique I have called "natural breathing." If we lock down our top ribs by squeezing our shoulder blades down our back, especially if we then draw down the sternum bone in the front, we cannot get a solid breath in.

Movement science describes this (especially the tensegrity model of anatomy). Once the ribs have full mobility and capture the ability to move all the way out and up from the top of the ribs to the floating ribs at the bottom of the ribcage, then the breath is free. Not only is the breath free, but so too the circulation frees up, we can begin to restore health to our pelvic floor—way at the bottom of our bodies, and our organs can properly detoxify. Breathing detoxifies the organs because when we inhale, our primary breathing muscle, the diaphragm, contracts and moves down toward the belly, which pressurizes the organs of digestion and elimination. When we exhale, sending the diaphragm back up toward the heart and away from the belly, the organs depressurize. This is a squeeze and release process that helps everything in the belly move, nourish, release, clean, and revitalize.

If you're not an anatomy geek like I am then simply learn how to follow the natural breathing exercises that I give and you'll go a long way to feeling a heck of a lot better in your body. Your body is worth it. The breath is a miracle.

The Pelvis

We return to the earliest written texts: the Sumerian cosmogenesis. In Babylonian myth the great goddess Tiamat was the mother of the gods and also the great salty sea. Tiamat and her consort Apsu, fresh water, joined to create the world, which was full of watery chaos. One of her descendants, Marduk, who was likely also the god of thunderstorms, eventually went to war with Tiamat. In order to go to war with her, however, Marduk demanded total authority over the gods. It was granted. This creation story, called the *Enuma Elish*, unfolds as a graphic and violent story of war, culminating in a vivid victory for Marduk. The thunder god goes to war against the mother, and he wins.

Marduk pierces Tiamat in the heart with his arrow and then cuts her in half down the middle, "like a fish for drying." From here he creates the known world out of her body, using her two ribs to create East and West, her liver to create the pole star, her curled tail to fashion the milky way. Finally, her pelvis becomes a support that holds up the sky. Of all the things to focus on in this story (and there's a lot), what stands out to me most is the image of the great mother's pelvis holding up the sky. It makes me think of how we sit, stand, and lie on this great earth. The sky, the infinite, needs to be held up by this foundation.

In modern perceptions of the yogic or tantric body, the pelvis is where the subtle energy resides. Specifically, the spiritual energy of the human is described as a serpent coiled three and a half times around the tailbone, with her mouth pointing upward, waiting to spring up and become the straight line of the body's awakened central axis. This serpent is also a goddess. Her name is Kuṇḍalinī. Originally kundalini was described as a coil or a sprout in the heart, or as the bent one called Kubjikā, but nowadays she is envisioned almost exclusively in the deep pelvis.

We have a lot going on where the pelvis meets the spine. A lot of nerves connect to this area- including nerves that deal exclusively with the body's ability to heal, rest, and digest food. Between the two halves of the pelvis sits a part of the lower spine called the sacrum. The word sacrum means "sacred bone." This triangle shaped bone lives just above the tailbone. It sits at the center of gravity for the body, creating shock absorption between the upper half of the body and the lower half of the body. Gravity and physical weight funnel upon the sacrum, which responds to this constant tension by rotating, moving forward, down, and back. It doesn't only take big movements to create this dance at the sacrum. When we breathe the sacrum moves also. It creates a ripple in the spine, which sends a rhythm through the fluids of the body and into the brain. The tantric texts that describe kundalini really do understand something of the physiological containing the mystical: the base of the pelvis contains our coiled core, from which and to which pulsation is expressed. The sacrum is sacred indeed.

When I lead trauma informed workshops and trainings, I usually focus on bringing movement back to the pelvis. I think of the pelvis as the place in the body where the physical meets the energetic. It is where embodiment expresses divinity. The pelvis experiences extraordinary pleasure when it allows this pulsation and extraordinary pain and trauma when it is violated. The pelvis is where trauma work meets tantra. It is where the serpent of the coiled universe holds up the sky of the infinite.

How Thoughts and Emotions Impact the Body

Everything we experience has a specific location in the body where it is held or where it resonates. The sacrum shows us this. Abreactions show us this. The process starts well before the trauma response. The thought-emotion layer of the heart interweaves with the physical heart and the body collective. The body responds immediately to thought-emotion. As soon as we start thinking and feeling we feel the amplification in our physical body. This is the interplay between the physical layer of the heart and the thought-emotion layer of the heart.

People, including doctors and therapists, understand this link.

When we are upset, our allies tell us to take a deep breath. This is wise advice. As I mentioned, strong emotions make us hold our breath, breathe quickly and shallowly, tighten our stomachs, override our biological needs for rest, digestion, and elimination of toxins in the body. Thought-emotions can be so disruptive in our lives that they cause us to stop eating, eat too much, lose sleep, or want to sleep all day. Thought-emotions can increase our stress hormones, increasing our cortisol levels.

Epigenetic research reveals that this is how stress can be passed onto our children. The work of Resmaa Menakem explores this topic through the lens of intergenerational trauma, racial justice, and how the body's experiences are carried forward into future generations. This is part of understanding ancestral trauma. In other words, thought-emotions create signals in the body. Scientists talk about stress as a dangerous and silent killer. This stress can be passed on through subtle hormonal signals, like more cortisol production, between a mother and her fetus, making the child and then the adult born of this mother more prone to anxiety or depression. Stress is the direct impact of the thought-emotion complex on the physical body.

Stress from thought-emotions is slightly different from inflammation, where the body is responding to stress from the outer environment. Even in this case, however, once the body is experiencing stress there is still an agitation in the thought-emotions related to that physical heat. The outer world impacts this chain just as much as the inner world.

Keeping the body healthy and clean is part of almost all religious traditions, and is usually one of the first things that the religion will command. This is because the physical health of the body can help or limit our investigation into thought-emotion. Being sick can stop our self-inquiry from the very start. The body matters when we investigate the mind.

To say that thoughts and emotions are somehow held apart from the body is to ignore our lived experience. All we need to do is look at the explosion of anxiety and depression in our culture to see that our thought patterns, those deep spirals of desire and craving we discussed above, torment us to a degree that impacts our ability to live comfortably in our own skin.

Start Here

When we are processing a big thought or emotion, we usually want to start with that thought or emotion, which isn't helpful a lot of the time. It's better to start with the body when we are processing. When we refer to big emotions, we can open the door to conversations around the body. We can say "I am really feeling angry in my jaw," and this simple acknowledgment can distribute the heat of the anger more evenly through our system and make us feel whole. It can even dissipate the thought spiral or emotion loop.

Every child I have observed doing this practice gains deep emotional intelligence, sovereignty, and validation by including their body in the naming of a thought-emotion. When we say to our children, "Where do you feel that feeling in your body?" they will tell us, "I feel it in my chest" or "I just want to jump and scream."

Ok, let's move our legs and lungs! Let's shake our arms! Including the body in the thought-emotion continuum is important, though we often leave it out of the picture. The body is by far the most capable and effective part of the chain at moving the energy in the chain—the thought or the feeling—if we engage it skillfully. It can make us feel extremely empowered, whole, and seen when we include all three aspects of our complete felt experience.

I think of thought-emotion-body as one single energy chain with three harmonizing notes. Depending on where I am experiencing an activation, which may be in any one of the three vibrational categories, I can identify and feel how that activation radiates out into the whole complex. If a shaming thought comes in, I can feel it move along that continuum into my emotions and body. On the other hand, if I stop breathing or notice that my stomach is in knots, I can travel that feeling back along the same chain and into a hidden emotion and thought. This should not be misunderstood. These are not three separate experiences but one single experience in interlocking harmony called by different names depending on where or how we notice what we notice. These are the outer two layers of the heart in near-constant play.

It is possible to have feelings and sensations in the body that touch us lightly enough to not ring as an emotion or thought. Sometimes touch is innocent: a yearning for warmth when we are cold or coolness when we are hot, unfettered by big emotions or thoughts. The point is not that every single body sensation connects us to a strong or overt emotion. The body is, after all, living in a dynamic world. It must respond to that world. But every sensation that catches our attention in patterns of gripping, bracing, and tightening, grabbing onto the world or rejecting the world, does contain an emotion. All stress contains emotion. All stress contains thought. We must learn to acknowledge that and track the message. If a sensation catches or snags, exhibits pain or contraction, it may be wise to stop and see what story the body is telling us. There are troves of information and recognition hidden in plain sight—or rather, in plain feeling.

Sensations to Pay Attention to as Body Notes

Pay attention to your body when it contracts: when the shoulders ache from gripping or there is a point of pain in the heart; when your breath is shallow and rapid; when your chest is tight or when you clench your jaw; when you pull in your arms to protect or cover yourself, or when you tighten your armpits; when your stomach squeezes and you lose your ability to listen to your natural eating needs by anxiously avoiding food or eating out of compulsion.

Pay attention to your body when it expands: when the collar bones spread like open wings; when the breath is free and the sounds of digestion are relaxed and audible; when there is a brightness in your eyes or under your skin; when you can make eye contact with a stranger or a loved one; when you are ungripped in the deep of your belly or unclenched in the space under your ears.

It takes a long time to look at our hidden transactions and to reconcile ourselves as being enough in our own hearts. If we stay curious about ourselves, we might start to see that life has come to our doorstep exactly because we are worthy of receiving its lessons. Just how we are. We are not perfect, but that is why we have so much good material to sandpaper against our hearts.

We have exactly enough rub there to turn up our earnestness if we decide to get down to business and listen to the heart. It's not easy, as I have said before. It's the hardest thing we can possibly do as humans. But at a certain point, the pain of not paying attention is more acute than the pain of paying attention. We do not want to keep living numb to our pains and desires. It takes a lot of energy to anesthetize ourselves, and to have to engage in that project of active avoidance daily is just exhausting. All the material used to create our character structure must be kindling for the fire, because the divine dance of emptiness creates all aspects of our personal selves, maintains them, and destroys them. We can choose a kindling that feels painful but we can also choose a starting point that feels expansive and beautiful. Both options are here. Listen to intuition to see which practice meets this moment.

We Are Verbs

We may begin through this process to see that our being is more like a verb than a noun—not a fixed person with fixed characteristics and roles but instead a fluid and constantly changing force that we can't pin to one expression, not even a solid body. Every time we eat, we change our body.

There are more neurons in our brain than stars in the Milky Way. Our body is creating and destroying, respectively, two million red blood cells every second. The changeover that happens every moment in the physical body is mind-boggling. Every aspect of our being is in constant flux. We are not in charge of this incredibly rapid action. None of us knows what our next thought will be. This is a good thing!

When my mother had a stroke, she reverted to deep and ancient thought patterns and ideas that had become fixed in her thoughts from an early age that clung to ego permanence. She said to me one day when she believed that she was dying, "When I go, I'll be in heaven, and from there, I can look down upon you forever!" Curious, my response was, "Do you think it's heaven to be yourself–forever?" After a moment of thought, she said, "Gosh, actually–no. That wouldn't be very much fun." That in us which is silent is eternal, but that in us which moves is always changing, including the ego. We love to think of ourselves as fixed–we even love the idea of staying ourselves somehow after death–forever. Forever with the same family, with the same self. If we spend even a moment thinking about this concept critically, we realize that it does not sound much like peace at all!

Our ability to shift, change, deepen, dissolve, recreate, adapt, and listen are true gifts. Mystery is a gift. This is the wobble that is resilience. This is how we allow ourselves to fall in all directions. This is how water binds to the dust particle and creates life-giving and life-sustaining rain. We never know what will happen next–and the birthing of possibility in all moments lets us source the intelligence of the vast stillness at our center- something that we cannot possibly know, plan, or fix.

When we try to stop and figure out what our next thought will be, we're either totally surprised by what comes up, or the mind simply gives up and goes quiet because it realizes it has no clue. It has no idea, literally. This can be kind of a fun game to play. Every once in a while, you can stop and get curious and wait for what thought could possibly come up next. Try it now. Ask yourself, *What will my next thought be?*

Every direction the body takes is an action, and even our thoughts and emotions are in constant spontaneous movement. Most of the time we do not know where that movement is leading. Nor do we know what the body will do next. We might have a really great plan to go for a run and even get our shoes on, get the music organized, and head out on the road. But things can change even with the best preparation–the body gets a cramp, that bothersome knee feels a twinge, the road is closed, or we get a phone call that we need to pick up our sick child from school. Even our most rehearsed plans are fluid.

A Practice

Notice what you notice.

1. **Pay Attention to Your Body.** Even the little things. Start to write them down, or pause and take note of how you feel in your breath and body. If something big comes up you can write it down and either take a look at it or simply leave it alone for the time being. Begin to address the many little hooks and reactions that don't feel quite so big. Like lifting weights, this exercise is most effective when you start with smaller weights and not with the huge traumas and heavy arguments. Build your strength, curiosity, and resilience.
2. **Discover Bartering Statements.** Are there any transactional statements buried in your experience of your body? Is there a way that you are saying to your experience: *I would be happy if...* Write down your transactional thoughts and see if you are bartering your heart. If this is enough to illuminate your thought process then simply ponder the peace of your heart in this moment.
3. **Feel What You Feel.** If there are deeper patterns that come up and carry memories, thoughts, or sensations in your body, pay attention to the sensations that arise. If there is a strong memory or emotion and no sensation in your body, turn toward your body and try to access the body element of your experience. Feel what you feel.
4. **Practice Natural Breathing.** I teach a technique that I call "natural breathing." This is less of a technique and more about reminding the physical body about the power of its own anatomy.

   Sit upright as much as you can so that your pelvis is not tipped forward too far or back. If this is difficult, lie on your back, bend your knees, and place your feet flat on the floor about hip width apart. This will allow your spine to be in a long line. If your spine is tender, you can place folded blankets underneath your back.

Place your hands on the sides of your ribs, up high under your armpits, and breathe wide into your hands until you can feel your side ribs move outward. Once the ribs are moving, make your exhalation just a little longer than your inhalation. If you can inhale for three or four counts, then try to exhale for five or six. Keep this going for as long as you are curious.

After a few breaths, artificially hold the ribs wide after a full inhalation. When you exhale, you will notice that your diaphragm muscle, which makes up the floor of your ribcage (or the rooftop of your belly), moves *back and up* more powerfully. Try it again. Inhale and artificially hold your ribs wide as much as you can while you exhale. Again, feel that your belly goes up and toward your heart.

Most of us exhale and push our bellies back into our spine. If we slump, drive a lot, sit a lot, or tuck our pelvis under, this exhalation will nearly always go back into the spine. Think of the abdominal exercise teacher saying, "Push your belly button to the back of your body!" We do not want to exhale in this way, because it compresses the vertebrae of the spine. For that matter, we do not want to exercise in this way either! If you learn to move your belly back and UP toward your heart then you can ignore your exercise teacher (or better yet, educate them about proper breathing).

When your rib cage is wide enough side-to-side to move freely, return to breathing so that your ribs expand up and away from your spine and then soften back down and in. However, stay mindful of your exhalations so that you do not push your belly button back toward your spine, but instead allow this J-shaped exhale that moves a tiny bit back but mostly up, like the little crook and the long line of the J.

CHAPTER 6

The Thought-Emotion Layer

WE GET STUCK on the layers of the heart, thinking we are only this one thing or that other thing. Each layer has its own ego traps. The ego lives on the thought-emotion layer of the heart, where it takes up its observations of all of the other layers and then weaves them into our beliefs and feelings.

I lovingly call my ego "the measuring stick." Of all the ways the ego is defined, described, and analyzed, seeing the ego as simply the measuring stick keeps things straightforward and honest. Let's acknowledge right away that the ego is often the villain in the spiritual saga. This is true for anyone who does not apply curiosity to the ego's mechanism. However, in this analysis, the ego is much more than a villain, which certainly is one role that it plays. We will see that the ego is also an ally, a friend, the dance of the Goddess, the one that climbs the layers of the heart and into the total recognition of our being. It can be an antihero, a jokester, and a helpless fool.

It is also only a measuring stick. Sometimes I find it helpful to pretend I'm carrying around a giant ruler when my ego comes out and starts tallying things up and down its scale. Like many parents, when my children were young, I printed out a large ruler onto one of our doorways to measure their growth. Depending on how quickly they sprouted up, we would periodically measure their new height and laugh, clap, or gasp at the changes over a few weeks, months, or seasons.

It is natural for us to measure our growth, to monitor our change, and to keep track of where we compare to those around us. Like all tools, this need to measure has its beauty and its darkness. We have talked a bit about ego traps already and have begun to see the ways that we slip into deeper ego patterns that bind us, but we have not yet investigated what, in fact, the ego is up to- how it works.

How the Measuring Stick Works

The ego is a hierarchy machine. The ego lives on the thought-emotion layer of the heart. It visits all of the layers of the heart to bring home its assessments. Still, thoughts and emotions are its home, where the ego makes its bed, gets up in the morning, and wanders around most of the day proclaiming things in better-than's and worse-than's.

What the ego does best is compare: it measures us against other people and situations. It also measures us against ourselves in clips of time, in thought, in emotion, and in worthiness. When I started talking to my inner measuring stick, I began to see that this mechanism that tallies me up and down is almost always self-referential.

I'm not good at this.

This used to not bother me, but now it does.

This used to bother me, but now it doesn't.

The ego even comments on our silence, saying, *You are less peaceful today than yesterday*.

A more complete sentence to these thoughts would be, *I'm not good at this compared to that person or to how I used to be when I was younger.* It's amazing how many statements we make to ourselves all day long that are comparisons. If we complete our thought sentences, which we're beginning to see is a huge part of the Goddess path, they are often either transactional statements or comparisons—and almost always both.

The measuring stick is far larger than transactional thinking, which is only one of its mechanisms, but because we give away much of our joy in bartering our heart, it's important to see that only the ego makes the bargain. The ego compares anything to anything, but in transactional thinking it hurts itself the most.

Like markings on a doorway, I know when I'm using my measuring stick pretty quickly now because every measurement I make in my thoughts, actions, and emotions is a signal that I am playing along with the game of ego.

We use the body all day long to measure things. We measure food as packets of energy. We measure the distances we move in minutes and miles. We measure other people and their spiritual progress, emotional availability, and skill at their career position. When we gather or enter a community, we either bond with people by measuring ourselves or our beliefs against them and coming to similar or at least compatible belief agreements, or we reject people because they measure unfavorably. Sometimes, we determine that people are below us intellectually, so we write them off as coarse or stupid. Sometimes, we see people as below us spiritually, calling them "unconscious." Sometimes we consider people above us in one of those categories, which is intimidating.

Very rarely do we fall in love with people based on the humanity that they shine through their simple presence, either because that presence is shielded by their own patterns, measurements, and ego, or because our presence is shielded by the same mechanisms. When we fall in love with people based on a hierarchy along the measuring stick, we are creating a precarious and ego-driven construct that is brittle and unstable. When, on the other hand, we fall in love with people because they are vast temples holding their own heart, we can't help but see beauty in all things.

If we spend all of our time in our activities holding up the great measuring stick then we are truly lost in a process that is out of our control, externalized, and agitating. This does not happen only in the marketplace and workplace. The hierarchy of spiritual experience captures our obsessive fascination more than almost any other project that the ego takes on, especially when the ego starts to sense that we contain layers of being where it has no job, no reach, and no entry.

I Can't Hang Out with Those People

One of the ego traps that I know most intimately, see most frequently in others, and find most difficult to move through, is the one that states: I just can't be around *those* kinds of people. Just like bigotry, the obvious expression of this statement, we can look at the subtle spiritual flavor of this trap because it's everywhere. This is one of the ways that the ego reaches down from the thought-emotion layer of the heart and into the energetic and intuitive layers, or even the void layer of the heart.

The words come out something like: "I only hang around people who are conscious." "That person is so unconscious I can't be near them." "I need to be around people who have the same high vibration I have." I've even heard, "I don't associate with muggles." When we are engaged in dogmatic religion, the statements are even more stark: "Those people can't be saved" or "I'm so lucky because I understand God and they don't." I have heard every one of these statements offered up with real conviction inside a spiritual context.

While it is important to distance oneself compassionately from people who genuinely cause us pain, toxic interactions, or violence, there are no people who are unconscious. Everyone is conscious. Think about what that word means. *Unconscious*. What we usually mean is that we believe (it's always a belief) that those people are less infinite than we are, less complete, or less whole, especially when we use the term spiritually. In other words, they are not about to transcend this whole planet and blink out in a spiritual ecstasy of perfection. Guess what? Neither are we. Everyone is following the path back to their own hearts, albeit at times blindly or clumsily or painfully. It's on us to have healthy boundaries and not on them to change their fundamental being.

We do not need the whole world to change so that we can move more freely. We do not need everyone else's behavior to clean up in order to develop more compassion, acceptance, and spaciousness within our own hearts. And yet, isn't this essentially what most of us are doing all day long? We are saying to our loved ones, "once you change your behavior, we can have a relationship," or, "if you get more conscious, I can be your friend again."

This is classic transactional relating. Using our bartering model, this sentence reads, "I will find love in my being when you raise your vibration to the same high frequency as mine, and we can enjoy that space together." We have bartered our hearts again. Does it really make sense to wait for someone else to become more conscious for us to find happiness?

When we subtly reject people we meet because they are not part of our club or church or belief group, or we reject most of the members of our family because their "vibration" is lower than ours, we are in acute spiritual arrogance territory. We measure and find them wanting while feeling pretty good about ourselves because we are "better." Feeling compassionate toward someone locked in destructive habits and pain might mean keeping that person at a wise distance without flare or pomp or resentment.

When we roundly reject others because of their limitations and pain bodies we are rejecting those qualities within ourselves. We are losing our resilience, our healthy wobble. The curious heart can hold space for all beings with tenderness, compassion, and concern, without needing that person to be our idea of better than they are and also without needing that person to hang out in our homes where we want to be quiet and peaceful.

Triggers Are Activations

The measuring stick appears most strongly when it gets activated. Activations are when something strongly plucks at us, hooking into the fabric of our perception, and saying, *Look!* Pay attention to that call: *Look at this!* When we get bothered, hot, or painful in our mind, body, or emotional field we are activated. There is a contraction.

Some people call this a *trigger*. I often try to avoid this word since it is violent and relates most often to weapons. At other times, it indicates that something has already happened and we can't stop it because it has been let loose and it's flying. Let's call it an "activation" instead, because it's not violent and the energy that calls at us is not out of our control. It can always be traced and followed, even while it's hot, carefully and at a pace that works for us. As an activation, we can follow the intelligence of the body's sensation. We can get somatic and interested in the field of awareness. We can get through the cracks of the measuring stick and into places where hierarchies collapse. An activation is a reflection in the mirror of the heart calling to us to get curious.

The city in the mirror is pointing out a street by lighting it up. This calling is the heart itself snagged against some experience. We can follow our thoughts, emotions, and physical body to something brilliant in that city. Sometimes this is a thought we are holding in our heart, a need, some kind of inner wisdom that we are trying to communicate to ourselves, or some error in our understanding of the situation that we find ourselves defending. At other times, it takes layer by layer of various activations to see the one tap root, like a mint plant that springs up all over the yard but has a wide underground network. Mint plants are hard to pull up because they are so great at building underground networks. Sometimes an activation is like this and we need to be patient and follow those roots until we get to the source.

Think back to the famous Greek myth of Narcissus. We usually remember the part where Narcissus stares at his reflection in the pond and falls in love with himself, with his tremendous beauty. But the story also involves a talkative mountain nymph named Echo and it is equally her story. Cursed by Hera (for being too chatty), Echo was only able to repeat another's words, to finish a sentence started by someone else. In this desperate state she saw Narcissus, a self-centered and beautiful young man, and fell in love with him instantly.

She followed him and wished for him and wanted to speak to him but because of her curse could only repeat back his words. Alone in the woods, Narcissus called out, "Is anyone there?" Echo repeated the words. Surprised, Narcissus said "Come here!" and she repeated the same. Emboldened, she approached him. When Echo and Narcissus finally came face to face, he rejected her and she fled, running from his insults. This did not stop her love.

After rejecting Echo, he became cursed by the gods as well: to fall in love and not be reciprocated just as she had been. This is how Narcissus found his own reflection in the waters, with Echo still whispering his own words behind him, causing him to feel that he had made a connection with this remarkable reflection. Finally, Narcissus died into his reflection, with her whispering his words in the background, both wasting away in unreciprocated love.

Our activations are like echoes. Some original call in our system, some original wound, is struck and then answered in resounding echoes whispering in many places throughout our mind, emotions, and body. We feel something and our reactive system calls it back to us insistently and in other places. If we do not turn toward our echoes, we might fall in love with the stories that they whisper. We might believe our thoughts, thinking they are real. We might think that we are thinking our thoughts. We might defend or go to war over our thoughts.

Until we can see the original curse that created the separation, the first wound that divided wholeness into sound echoes and obsessive love of the bouncing reflection, that compulsive need to follow our thoughts and reactions for days and years and decades, our faces only turned toward the reflection, then we will be fundamentally divided by our yearning to touch love but cursed to chasing echoes.

Whatever the activation says will surely reveal itself if we listen closely. It is a word, a phrase, a belief, a body sensation, an emotion, or all of these. If we do not listen, then the activation will likely come back again and again. Feeling our feelings can be painful, but there is immense joy and relief in the feeling.

In the path of the Goddess, spiritual practice and psychology become deep lovers because psychology reveals the echoes of the mind, the way to trace the echoes, and the curses that create the patterns. And spiritual practice brings that inquiry through the nested layers of the heart, giving dignity to all of the layers and honoring the echoes as a kind of calling home into life. The echoes and the obsessions that we carry resolve into one another when the original wound is understood totally. But we must learn to understand how our activations happen, and we must develop the tools to listen. That's part of the curious path, too.

Get Activated

The smallest daily activations in our lives are often the most beneficial mirrors to see our patterns, offering us huge wellsprings of insight when we turn toward the fissures of reactiveness. Letting the outer world knock against our thoughts and emotions creates real feedback that is useful and important.

My husband once dropped our son off at school and returned frustrated because a mom was blocking everyone in the drop-off line, waving to people, going around the drop-off line several times in her car, and generally making a show. At first twitch, it is easy to say, "That person is so unconscious." But upon investigation, when we are hot and bothered, it is our own selves we are not seeing clearly.

This small experience activated my husband in two ways: he wanted to drop off our son on time so as not to be late, and he did not appreciate the delay. Compounding that, the woman's general showiness with her jewelry dangling out the window of her big car made her seem entitled and imposing. The deeper activation came from childhood impressions: a need to be on time for him was a constant measure of success and goodness, and his family culture severely judged showiness and peacocking as snobbish and rude.

The experience brought up two core memories for him, but upon investigation those memories belonged to deeper family anxieties, judgments, and impressions of how people ought to be, how they should behave, how they should tuck in their heads and just move on. "We should always blend in and be good" might be the core thought, and the full sentence might be, *I would be happy if everyone were just polite and inconspicuous.* Once we see the deeper thoughts, the experience loses its charge and becomes innocent, even a little humorous. Our deeper sense of right and wrong often totally blocks the innocence of a moment.

Daily frustrations help us see our judgments and impressions because spiritual inquiry and continuous personal experience work hand in hand, and on this path of turning-toward the heart, the work is inevitably related to understanding separation and pain. When we begin to see the painful stories that we carry it can feel overwhelming. The point here is to create a container for the experiences you are probably already having and may not have the tools or the perspective to dive into.

We need organization when we are doing the work of inner illumination, especially when it feels like everything is being activated all at once. We need to look at our stories one at a time so that we can appreciate and digest the lessons. Each one is a reflection in the mirror.

We carry simple small activations, larger ones that seem to block us, and the cul-de-sac activations that keep us turning in one place. We stop letting it go and start inviting it in. When this happens the content, substance, and experiences of life do not change—the path that walks us into the heart is the same path that takes us out- but we find that living our self-noticing, our reflective awareness, is well worth the whole experience.

Thought-Emotion

The measuring stick creates hard lines between our thoughts, emotions, and body. We routinely put each of these experiences into separate categories. However, this separation of forms is simply not true to our lived experience when we take a look. The only reason we call them separate is because we just haven't noticed and because there's no word in English for one function called *thought-emotion.*

Thought and emotion are so connected that they are one unit of experience. In the yoga traditions there is only one word that describes both thought and emotion, *citta*, acknowledging that thought is no different from emotion. *Citta* sometimes means simply mind, but it means mind in the sense of what moves. Thought. Emotion. Both.

Almost every thought we have ever had contains a kernel of emotion. A thought that tries to stand apart from emotion strikes us as distancing or frightening. We call people who are capable of having thoughts that they remove from their emotions dry, humorless, or calculating. In extreme cases we call this sociopathic behavior. This is *extreme thought.*

It's unnerving to have thoughts that feel removed from emotion because we know instinctively that we can't remove thought from emotion. It takes a tremendous amount of effort and energy to remove a thought from its associated feelings. This causes pathology and pain. We don't tend to feel at ease around people who show no emotions, but move through thoughts mechanically. Likewise, we modulate every emotion by thought. When an emotion feels strong, this thought or family of thoughts can spin in dizzying and repetitive circles. Like extreme thought, we find people who have emotions without awareness of the associated thought to be dangerous. That's what it means to "really lose it." We might say, "That person had a moment of blind rage" or "They can't get a grip on reality." These are examples of *extreme emotion.*

Emotional women used to be labeled "hysterical." Hysteria is in fact the first diagnostic label given to women to describe mental disorder, going back almost 4,000 years. It was associated with sorcery, demonology, sexual aberrance, and—by the time Freud got around to describing it—was an exclusively female problem. The extremely emotional and traumatized person, especially the female, has always been regarded as dangerous.

We can even identify our emotions by thoughts that return over and over again. The thought, *I need to go to the grocery store*, is fairly simple, carrying a relatively easy emotion that might be a spark or feeling of satisfaction at being responsible, a feeling of frustration at not having enough time, or a feeling of anxiety. Sometimes, we do not notice these feelings at all. But if we were to think, *I need to go to the grocery store* over and over again, then we begin to see the emotion under the thought.

We might take the longer pathway elaborating that original thought, *I need to go to the grocery store*: "Why am I always the one that goes to the grocery store? My partner could totally go, but of course, he never helps me out. It's all on me. And I am always the one who needs to cook for the family, but I just don't have the time and the energy. I don't even know what to make. I have ten other things on my plate, but now I have to go to the grocery store because we're running low on the only type of yogurt my partner will eat in the morning."

This is now an emotion that has spun the original thought into a whole world of anxiety, resentment, and anger. It's subtle to see when a thought amplifies into an emotion. Still, when we are way deep into an emotion, we can usually trace it back to an original thought, and in my experience, there are only a few core thoughts that spring outward into emotion. When we follow our activations through our thoughts and emotions, we begin to notice something. Anger almost always shields sadness or grief. Sadness shields fear. Fear shields a core thought around worthiness, like: *I am not worthy of being loved; I am not good enough*; or *I'm not worthy of being seen*. Unworthiness is often the core thought that blooms into most of our reactive emotions. We are so fused in our thoughts and emotions that we often do not realize how interdependent those two forces are or where the one slips into the other.

Non-Attachment

This is why many traditions practice non-attachment as one of the first lessons in cleaning up our disorganized and desire-driven minds. Non-attachment means releasing the bargain. The problem is that most patriarchal traditions don't teach non-attachment at all, but rather a form of transcendent disassociation which is often harmful, confusing, or simply unattainable. It is possible and necessary to bring the wisdom of non-attachment into the lived experience, especially in family dynamics and relationships. It is possible to see the heart clearly at all times of our existence.

I misunderstood non-attachment for so long that I expressed a whole arc of responses to the teaching. I went through my good student phase (I call her Hermione), where I tried my best to be non-attached to the things I loved. I went through a phase after having children of rebellion and anger at the concept, thinking, *It's easy enough for you teachers to sit on a mountaintop without family or children and preach non-attachment! But how do you expect me to do that? I have a baby that relies on my body and my quick responsiveness to stay alive every hour of the day! I won't do it.*

After long and deep practice, the teachings of non-attachment started to become clearer and I became less reactive. That's the whole point. Non-attachment means becoming disinterested in reacting to the content of the world. It means no longer bartering the heart for anyone or anything. The heart becomes too valuable to simply give away.

Non-attachment practices also live on the thought-emotion layer of the heart, and exploring this common spiritual lesson is useful because we can start to see how the patriarchy has appropriated it. Non-attachment does not mean renunciation. We mix the two topics mercilessly. Renunciation, where we remove ourselves in body and communication entirely from society and follow the monk's path, is an extreme path of non-attachment built from the patriarchal model of religion and tradition.

Non-attachment is not always a path of renunciation. When we include the Goddess, we are not taught to renounce. Instead, we are called to stay exactly where we are, complexities and all, and work on disentangling our desire mechanisms in the middle of the busy human life. Non-attachment for a person who is engaged in life, has relationships, uses the body in those relationships to hug and make love and touch, and walks the path of someone with family, friends, community, and work, is all about taking the transactional impulse out of the picture. It means not being whiplashed by our bargaining agreements—the forms of desire like anticipation, worry, nostalgia, and shame.

When the bargaining begins, we can train ourselves to see it. We can even amplify our bargaining statements in order to understand where they come from and where they are going, and we can decide if the agreements are helping us. Practicing non-attachment well in a busy life is extraordinarily freeing. It means that we are free to love the ones that we love. It means we meet every situation of life fresh instead of showing up at the table with a debt to pay or be paid.

Nothing on the outside needs to be changed or renounced. When this happens, we see the whole world as the unfolding of ourselves in the mirror of our heart. We see our relationships as a reflection of the divine. The city in the mirror is a lot more dynamic and the reflection is clear. We no longer subscribe to tit-for-tat agreements with our partners and loved ones that become always more complicated and full of resentment and that so often collapse those very relationships.

I find it unfortunate that entire cultures say, "you can have a family while you are still developing, but once you're ready to be mature you must devote yourself to a *real* spiritual practice by becoming a monk and taking yourself away from all these worldly things."

The Buddha himself famously left his family—his wife and young children, his life as a householder in a palace—to become a wandering monk. He was born into an orthodox Brahmanical society which already contained the patriarchy of religion embedded within it, and so the religious ideal of his time was already entrenched in "let it go" spirituality. And he did *let it go*. He left his family in his late twenties, became awakened in his mid-thirties, and spent the rest of his life into his eighties teaching (almost exclusively male) monks out in the deep woods.

We have taken stories like this one and glamorized what it means to remove ourselves from family, life, and the distractions of things like children and their incessant needs. I am not suggesting that the Buddha himself did something wrong or unacceptable. His path was his own, and it worked for him within his time and place. But generations of people have fetishized that path and assumed, “If that is the way this great awakened being did it, then that is the path that’s best.” Then the teachings of whole religions build their models on that very path.

It’s not a universal. It is a path that worked for someone at some point in time (a really long time ago), in a society where the context of religious success was already entrenched (the patriarchal model). It worked for the Buddha. It worked for some other people in the Buddha’s lineage. But it is not universal, nor even the most effective path for the majority of people. If anything, this model has stopped or limited the deepening process of countless people who thought, *This is what I must do to know myself,* and so cut themselves off from their lives. What most people really need is the stimulation and reflection of life, relationships, and active engagement to cultivate the heart as whole. Transcendence models move us away from the actions of life, such as thoughts, emotions, sensations, perceptions, and sentience.

The results of this kind of thinking are disastrous in our practice, often making us dismissive of our fellow humans, including loved ones and family members, and stopping us from being compassionate actors in this life journey. We might even leave our families and friends in a totally sanctioned and “valid” expression of personal growth and spiritual mastery. We then spend a lot of time talking about what we are *not* and we spend very little time talking about what we *are* in the here-and-now.

When we seldom use the words of the heart, such as love, listening, acceptance, intuition, and vulnerability, we are closing off a part of ourselves. And not only us. We need to listen to the people on the path with us and the teachers we choose. It is important to listen to how often a teacher uses these terms or how often a teacher avoids them and instead focuses on the “you are not” terminology. If that is the case, take some time to investigate how this language makes you feel, how it feeds your heart or makes your heart contract, and how you intuitively feel about it. See if part of you is missing.

In these teachings, I often find myself thinking, *Ok, this is a good first half: What I'm not. But where is the second half of the lesson? When do we get to talk about what I am, and what I can turn toward?* The ratio of these terms tells us a lot about where a person, even a teacher, is on the path of the heart, no matter how much they claim to know or posture in the theater of their teachings. Moreover, if a teacher is causing pain in their personal world, it is worthwhile to stop and pay attention. A teacher who transmits deep peace and profound states of contemplation or ego dissolving but who has left schisms of pain in a living family circle must reassess the balance within their heart.

I know a deeply awake teacher whose words open us into the absolute peace of our being, but after decades of marriage, he left his wife for a young student suddenly and dramatically. This is not a new story. It's so old that we barely bat our eyes when we hear it. But it's not normal. It would be fine if there was an honest way to face the pain and a direct and involved process where all parties were allowed to communicate, to have the full breath of their experience. But when his previous partner is simply dropped to the side and left to feel her pain on her own then there is a major problem, and that problem impacts everyone involved. When we create pain, there is work to do.

Sweeping pain under the rug, especially under the guise of "none of this exists," is a corruption of spiritual practice. If there is plenty of communication, process, and honoring of separating paths, then that is a different story; all too often, however, these breaks in the personal lives of senior teachers cause real trauma in the ones left behind. We are not isolated units of awareness. We are reflections upon reflections of our hearts, and the images in those mirrors have meaning and depth.

If we leave our spouse for someone younger and more exciting, or if we abandon the ones we love by constantly traveling and teaching and making a name for ourselves, or if we hold workshops and retreats that cost a small fortune and enforce financial barriers to our teachings, driving off during the breaks in our shiny luxury car, then something is not embodied. We can definitely say something is incomplete when those nearest to us are in pain, left behind, or taken out of the process. The heart has been bargained away wherever there is pain left in our life's wake.

A Goddess Path Story of Non-Attachment

One story in the sacred text Yoga Vasistha shows us a balanced representation of deep non-attachment. In the story, there was a young king and queen who were happily married and dedicated to the kingdom and their spiritual process. They represented the spiritual and ethical ideal. The wife, Queen Chudala, became such a devotee of her path that she became enlightened. Her husband, King Sikhidvaja, noticed the changes in his wife and decided he wanted to pursue his spiritual path. In his mind, the only way to do this was to wander off into the forest and abandon his family, his home, and kingdom to discover his deeper calling. Understanding a bigger truth and from a place of profound wisdom, Chudala said to him, "Your work and your duty is here; stay! You do not need to leave everything to become self-realized." Of course, the king didn't listen. He called her a silly woman and ridiculed her. Off into the woods he went.

Months turned into years. He suffered terribly. In this amount of time, Chudala, who was enlightened and now also ruling the kingdom, practiced and developed special yoga powers which allowed her to take astral forms and travel wide distances. Using her magical abilities, she would go and visit her husband. She took the form of a young sage, someone that her husband could speak to and trust. Little by little, in the form of this young man, she pierced the veil and guided him into the total recognition of his heart. She convinced him to come home to her. And so it was that after twenty years of wandering, he returned to his kingdom and his wife, who was also his teacher in disguise, now fully realized but also more profoundly connected to his worldly duties.

The Goddess always brings her beloved home.

Every single one of us has a path and a purpose. Learning to walk that path and purpose with focused reverence and attentive dedication is a much more nuanced journey, but also a truer reflection of the heart.

A Practice

Notice what you notice.

1. **Identify the Ego.** I like to think of my measuring stick as slightly external to my body. This gives me a bit more perspective and just a hint of distance from the workings of the ego when things are difficult. It can feel painful to always feel the ego as internal. In order to make friends with the ego and really start to understand it, try externalizing it for a time and watching the ways that you tally yourself against yourself and others.
2. **Work on a Comparison.** Take one of the measurements that seems to grip you. This can be a simple yet persistent judgment, perhaps toward a relative, politician, or colleague.
3. **Take a recurring thought or a recent disappointment and write it down.** Identify what emotion is deeply connected to that thought. Write down the emotion next to the thought.
4. **Feel into the body:** how is my physiology responding to this thought-emotion? Does it impact my breath? Does it create a tightness, a pain, a fluttering, a knot, or a tensing somewhere? Does it make me feel sad? Angry? Betrayed? Where is that feeling in my body? How is my jaw responding? How is my stomach responding? What about my shoulders?
5. **Ask, is this judgment really true?** What does it activate in me that makes my heart feel this way?
6. **Contemplate Freedom from Comparison.** Either deepen into the pause naturally or cultivate that deepening by imagining all of your roles: your name, gender, age, relationships, profession, loves, hates, beliefs, and memories as part of a patchwork blanket that you wrap yourself in. Take your blanket off and place it in a

safe space next to you—it's there, you have not thrown it out—it's just folded neatly to your side or placed in an imaginary basket. What is it like to take off this cloth? What are you left with, and how do you feel?

CHAPTER 7

The Deep Intuition Layer

THE WAYS THAT we get stuck on the physical as well as the thought-emotional layers of the heart is being addressed more and more, and amazing therapists, scientists, and doctors are teaching us a lot about the mind-body connections. We also can get stuck at the intuitive layer. This is sometimes a more subtle or even a spiritual phenomenon, and it's something that is less investigated than some of the layers we have already looked at.

When I was twelve, I traveled with my family to Turkey, where my father grew up, and was up late at night with jet lag. I remember looking around the room in my slightly disoriented state—day was night, night was day, walls were different from my room at home. But what I saw through that fresh lens at two in the morning was immediate and complete—there was no essential difference in what I was looking at: nothing had a boundary. There were walls and furniture pieces, but there was no separation of those things as individual objects. All the objects in the room were suddenly one luminous subject—me. There were no edges to "my" awareness, and everything was One thing.

I did not have the language for this opening, and I couldn't exactly tell the people around me, "Hey, despite what you've been told, everything is One thing!" How does someone explain this, let alone a child? These experiences cannot be explained, but they do change us.

I knew that this was the simple Truth of Reality—that there is only One thing, probably that thing other people called God. Maybe. It didn't really fit, was the problem. I was a Jewish kid going to a Christian school. Not one book or hymn or teacher from either religion had yet said to me, "There are no edges to things—there is no such thing as separation. It's all one thing." Yet I knew I saw an edgeless, unlimited, luminous, and shining single reality when I looked out of my eyes.

Since I did not have a model for this truth, I made one up. I called this my new religion, and I named that religion One. I followed my own private little religion through my teen years and into young adulthood. My private religion did not have any practices, rules, or rituals, but I did stay on the lookout for that dissolution, feeling a little shimmer or a little dropping away here and there while I was living daily life. It didn't happen a lot, but it did seem that life was playing a game with me.

Sometimes I would have a dream, and some image from the dream (that book on the subway) would appear in the "real" world the next day. I got used to thinking about a person moments before seeing them, even if I had not seen that person in weeks or years. Life was joking around, and it felt good to laugh along.

I was primed to be spiritually curious, but I had more questions than I had answers.

Promiscuous Mystics

Then, when I was twenty-four, I had an energy awakening in an act of intimacy with my husband. My entire world shifted. The floodgates opened in a specific way that gave me a direct experience of unity consciousness, the way of Mother Reality. To this day, the floodgates remain open, though the currents have changed significantly with the years. This all happened one afternoon early in our marriage when we came together in such an open and intimate way, that from the moment we touched I felt a real, tangible torrent of electric energy flowing between us. The energy was a circle and it had no beginning and no end. There was nothing above and nothing below. There was only the circle.

What happened next cannot be described precisely, though I saw the entire dance of light and presence flowing through my husband and through me in a circle of archetypal masculine and feminine, and I saw the universe unfold with my heart as its eyes. I experienced hours of energy waves in and through my body and being without cessation or exhaustion. Orgasm through sex, through touch, through being, though not dependent whatsoever on any of those conduits. It was a unity of the masculine and feminine energies that included everything. The body and the earth. It was independent and free, needing nothing outside of itself, and utterly whole, available in all time.

When we have a transformational mystical experience, we want to shift our lives, the entire architecture of our existence, towards those possibilities. After my experiences of unity, I wanted to know more. I wanted to take on practices, learn traditions, and *do more* to have that experience again.

I was drunk on mystical experience, and I would do whatever I could to take a sip again. I had found the intuition layer of my heart where wild things danced and mysteries spun into incredible stories. Sometimes I turned toward more mystical and occult traditions, sniffing out energy healers, seers, visionaries, channelers, and psychics. Surely I could rub up against that energy again and again and experience more bliss, which I happily did for many years. I still carried that subtle image of the silent, wise man inside me but, hey, I could still get there if I did more. And doing more was sure fun!

Once again, I turned toward striving. I wanted more experience, more perfection, and any tradition that could unpack or give me another hit of the mystical pipe. I avoided the transcendence hangover by jumping into the next transcendent experience. Energy was my language. I believed a lot of things, until those beliefs fell apart, and I turned to a new belief.

Like many others, I became a retreat junkie—every chance I got I would try to rush off to study with a new teacher, absorb a new teaching, practice a new technique. Humans have been experiencing mystical and noetic states throughout our long history and sharing these experiences directly with others through transmission, story, and ceremony.

Abhinavagupta wrote, "For one on the path of divine intuition, there is no necessity for the procedure of the several initiations, no formal consecration as a guru, no necessity for lineage etc., and no ritual vow of mantras, since he is directed by the primal sage, the great God. It is for the attainment of such inner direction that all such rites are offered; but it is already his own nature."[11] Intuition is our nature. Of course, this does get reflected in our practices and sacred acts. Civilizations, mythologies, and day to day practicalities like how we choose to live and bury our dead reflect these types of experiences.

I started to feel like a super-charged electrical cord that was pulled out of the socket and was whipping around the room. My body was burning out and my nervous system was unhealthy. I began to live with the consequences of running too much electricity in a system that was too human to handle the load. Slowing down has revealed to me more of the depth of practice, including the layers of my own heart. It is in the slow investigation that we begin to uncover these layers, especially the energy self, finding bit by bit where we are still holding pockets of compulsion and how to shift the expression into reverence.

Lipstick Spirituality

With a fresh and quickly transforming modern culture that seems to be getting ever more fast-paced and more information-heavy, we seem to have lost the slow, deep contemplative pathways that have underpinned human culture. Slowing down is the only way into the intuitive layer of the heart. We must regain the ability to find one thing that works and then root into it with dedication and simplicity to get to the depth of our center, with devotion and reverence. It took me a long time to slow down, to turn inward, and get curious. That's when I started to discover the Goddess path. She was there in my own heart, trying to steer the ship with calm and precision, all while I was like a wild bucking ocean throwing spray in her face.

We tend to run circles around one layer of the heart, say the thought-emotion layer by going to therapy for decades but still feeling fits of rage and shame because we have never listened to the full sentences of our transactional thinking; or the intuitive layer by creating whole worlds of magic that feel more real than the skin that wraps around our delicate limbs. In the energy and intuition layer of the heart we can try to cover up our tracks by trying on a new color of lipstick, hoping that will be enough to get us by. We can even become experts at this one layer of the heart, spinning around and around and forgetting the rest. I call this *lipstick spirituality.*

Lipstick spirituality is one way that we hide in our deep inner practices—how we may become well-versed, or even advanced, in certain techniques or experiences, but we haven't seen our core material, scaled the heart from the innermost to the outermost, then from the outermost to the innermost, followed our activations, changed our painful behaviors, or become kinder to the ones we love (or hate) most. In many ways, becoming a "master" of a technique is extremely dangerous because expertise leaves little room for failure, growth, and process.

I have worn many shades of lipstick.

Like many westerners, I became quite promiscuous when it came to spiritual seeking. That loss of balance was instructive. I was teetering between my physical body, my thought-emotion layers, and deep intuition. These layers were unanchored from the silent core of my heart, and so I lost my wobble and became rigid. Rigidity and hidden ideals of perfectionism lead to lipstick spirituality.

We have two modern problems that create rigidity and pin us at the intuitive layer of the heart. Both of these traps are ultimately driven more by the glamor of spiritual practices and less by the real potential of those same practices. Understanding these two cul-de-sacs can allow us to reflect on the direction of our own paths and give us greater agency in determining how, why, and what we practice as we turn inward.

In lipstick spirituality we are more interested in becoming perfect—when we want to see a beautiful image in the mirror, rather than what life is really reflecting in the mirror. What life teaches us is complex and the Goddess holds the ability to get so big that we can become the cup that holds many opposites. This is beautiful and far more interesting than perfection. Lipstick spirituality can stop us from becoming the full instrument of the heart: the wide space of our expansive being.

The first of these two problems is this: we typically adopt these outside systems to improve ourselves or become more perfect *versions* of ourselves.

The self-help path

When we believe that our spiritual path, the Goddess path, will fundamentally help us on an individual or personal level to become more perfect, we're on the self-help path. This creates rigidity. It leads to all kinds of spiritual arrogance, ego-driven teaching, and abuse of power. The Goddess path sees the "self" as something quite fluid, multi-layered, requiring us to claim our wholeness with such a totality that, depending on our current activation or transactional thought, we might respond to this self in entirely different ways.

We love self-help. (You may even have discovered this book in the "Self-Help" section of a bookstore. Most bookstores don't yet have a Goddess section...) We genuinely want to become better people. We either want to become better people in order to improve our daily lives, or be happier in our human roles, or to facilitate better mystical connections. We love working with the tools that help us prioritize individual self-actualization, innovation, and personal improvement. Sometimes we wrap our spiritual practices in this language, especially when we have bought into the idea that we can perfect ourselves, and that the next hot thing might just be the ticket to that project of me-being-a-better-me.

We don't stop at self-help. We then try to package what we found inspiring within our unique perspective; to make a name for ourselves. We associate success with innovation and the "listen to me" voice. We want to discover something new and then brand it. The thinking is: "If I can become a better me, then I can create my own system that will help you become a better you." We want to write the book and then claim that book as original.

Nowadays we must be original. A scientific or spiritual theory can be hundreds of years old, but if we find a new take on it and then stamp our name on that insight, we will have succeeded in claiming our little corner of the universe. We will have proven that we are indeed the successful, best-version of ourselves possible. Then we market that self to the world, put our name on our new idea or way of being, and find success in our triumph of individuality in that new way. Truth is universal. We must simply gather the crumbs of truth how we can and to the best of our ability, investigating the thousands of years of brilliance that other humans have expressed before us. Isn't that a relief?

In many eastern traditions no new or unique perspective is considered valid unless it is anchored in conversation with traditional language, scripture, and establishment. If a teaching was not described or addressed in previous texts or teachings then it was not considered valid because it had not been substantiated by time, scripture, or tradition. For hundreds of years the yoga and tantra adepts who introduced new ideas in most sacred texts would try to downplay the innovation with a phrase like, "There is nothing new about this idea, it has been said many times before," or they explained it as a response to another ancient idea with which it was entwined. Scholars are pretty cued in and know that when this disclaimer starts a passage, it probably does contain new or modified material. But the teachers went out of their way to say, "This isn't new! I didn't make this up!" which is exactly the opposite of what we do today.

Individuality is simply not an imperative in all cultures. It is only in our cultural Eurocentric world that we market our new take on ancient perspectives, we make a name for ourselves, and we push for recognition in those insights. This is an outcome of the patriarchy. It is a race to the top, to the goal, to the transcendence of winning some small game of immortality.

In the West we can say the same thing someone else said yesterday and claim, "This is totally new, I made it up," in order to achieve our cultural definition of success. It's a brief immortality, but still we play the game. We have to do this to succeed within the model in which we live. This authorship attitude is fundamentally different in other traditions, especially and specifically those traditions that explore deep heart practices, the paths of the Goddess.

We do not need to own knowledge on the Goddess path. Knowledge is internal, intuitive, shared. In this process we are learning to take the material of the world—the reflections in the city in the mirror, the layers of our heart, and listen deeply. We are recalling all of ourselves and using our activations to turn toward whatever wants attention. When information arises then we follow the crumbs. This is a path of choosing reverence over compulsion until everything is reverence.

Success in the world can happen then. Success is inevitable then. Success is measured by how deeply we connect. Supporting ourselves and our family—this too is success, and this too is born of reverence. Success, when measured by reverence, changes the canvas of our experiences. We get to work when we need to get to work, and we even start to rest when we need to rest. The Goddess path, because it sits unwaveringly on the foundation of the heart, can change the whole architecture of our existence, weaving into our lives exactly as-is or changing nearly everything top-down.

We need help when we think we are broken. The Goddess path reminds us that we are not broken, and that we have never been broken. We are complex, full of contradictory and paradoxical truths, like pain and wisdom, dissatisfaction and peace.

When we reorient "self" and "help" on the Goddess path then we can actually turn toward the practices that will address what's happening here and now. Then self-help might take on a totally different meaning, because our definition of the "Self" and our definition of "help" have changed. Sometimes these practices come through a book or a teacher, and sometimes they come through someplace much quieter and more internal. In some cases, the practices that come through might seem very odd from the outside.

The "I'm not enough," the "I'm not worthy of love," the "I can't possibly hold this much power," the "I'm too broken"—hides under these wings that give rise to fear, then grief, then anger. When I finally saw this voice, and *oh it took me a long time to see this voice,* I realized it was built into the very fabric of my being. So I did something strange. I saw that I had an activation and it was almost always talking to me. The activation was subtle, deeply energetic, very quiet. So I spontaneously started to make the voice louder.

I began to breathe my unworthiness. I took it out into the world with me. I was not taught to do this—it just happened. Everywhere I went I brought my painful breath-speak with me. I spoke it out loud sometimes. For days, then weeks, over a month, I carried this voice—no longer buried but now at the front of my thoughts, into my life.

It was hard. It was so very hard. But the "I'm not good enough" was also seen, surprisingly quickly, to be a charlatan. I went to the grocery store and people smiled at me. The voice was lying to me. I went home and hugged my family. Someone said, "I love you." The voice was not telling me what was really happening on the ground in my life. The more I lived my life, the more this voice was seen to be untrue. I started to call this voice the liar, "*la mentirosa*" in Spanish, the language I spoke as a young child at home with my grandmother. So I let *la mentirosa* hang on for a while until she became quieter. Until she became really and truly seen. I did not let her go. I amplified her. I needed to turn toward this voice in a way that I could really understand her. And once she was seen through, she started to disappear. And one day, she was gone.

The voice that says "I'm not good enough" is lying to you. You are whole. You are good enough. You are more than enough. This is the way to see that the Self-Help path does not make us more worthy, does not make us more perfect, does not make us more whole. That's already here.

Take a moment to really and truly feel, even for a moment, that you are whole. I often tell students to rub their palms together and then place their hands on their hearts. You can do that now, and bow into yourself—all of yourself. Bow into the parts of yourself that you show to the world: the parts that you celebrate and claim. Bow into the parts of yourself that you hide from the world: the parts that you tuck away and try to forget. Bow into all of yourself.

The Spiritual-But-Not-Religious Path

The second problem of lipstick spirituality is one of context. We often don't understand (and don't want to understand) the historical, cultural, and religious context of the practices that we adopt. We don't appreciate how much background, priming, study, and lineage are involved in most meditative or self-inquiry religions and traditions globally and historically.

Calling something a tradition because it is different from our western notions of monotheistic religion does not negate the fact that most traditions we turn to when opening our intuition are in fact well-organized philosophies and religions, and practiced as such in their original forms. When we sit with a medicine in a circle, we are connecting to generations, perhaps thousands of generations, of humans who have a relationship to the circle. We are connecting to a lineage, a tradition, and a way of approaching ourselves that has rules, suggestions, and safety protocols.

All circles and communities are like this: there are rules, suggestions, and safety protocols. Spiritual practice is hard. It is a commitment. Almost all prayer, ceremony, or meditation-based traditions require intensive vetting, practice, ritual, and secrecy. The layers of the heart take time and understanding, and initiates have to follow specific practices to learn them, as in all religions.

We try to move toward foreign religion and away from our home culture religion, saying, "I'm not religious, I'm spiritual." Never mind that this nearly always means, "I'm not religious according to the religions of monotheism. I am now religious according to eastern or mystical or occult religions."

Such a large part of the population (nearly 25 percent in the U.S. alone) now identifies as spiritual but not religious (SBNR), and millions of others are exploring this category. I'd like to remind you that being spiritual *is* religious. Both terms indicate that we are curious about something inside. Something bigger than us. Something maybe that we can turn toward and get curious about in new ways. Most importantly, being spiritual does mean getting to work. It means hearing the song and following the music. That music is playing the strings of the heart. Being spiritual and being religious both require building networks of safety, care, and focus.

If we are unsafe in our spiritual practices, we risk spiritual crisis.

This is tamed in four key ways, called the four pillars to liberation in the Yoga Vasistha: through dedication to a path, cultivating inner contentment (which is different from happiness), engaging our self-inquiry, and finding a spiritual community. These four solutions to spiritual crisis mitigate the whiplash that can happen when we are spiritually promiscuous and can even save our sanity, if also our lives. Here they are laid out. The solution to spiritual crisis is this fourfold path:

1. Dedication to your practice: This expresses commitment to yourself. This is curiosity in your process.
2. Cultivating contentment: What you might call softness, welcoming, or inner space—that is contentment. It is not the bright lights of happiness, but something more subtle. The smile within the smile. This is curiosity of the moment. It is equanimity.
3. Engaging in self-inquiry: This is looking at the deep inner heart and following the path inward. This is curiosity of the innermost Self.
4. Spiritual community: Having a friend, a mentor, an ally, a therapist, or a group that makes you

> feel seen, safe, and that you can share your heart with. This is curiosity in sharing, in the group, in the network of hearts that connect to your heart.

A lot of times when we say we are SBNR, we're signaling that we've broken with the dogmas and practices of our personal, family, or culture's religious tradition. We think, *Religion isn't for me anymore.* We've let go of structure but we still hear the call of the heart. We have, in this case, begun to listen intently to our deep intuition layer of the heart, which means we have had to leave religions that focus intently on the body layer of the heart or on the body layer and the thought-emotion layer, but no more. Sometimes the intuition layer causes us to break with scriptures and teachers that do not sync with our intuition because we feel that these scriptures and teachers cannot give our heart its wisest reflection. When we prioritize our intuition, we take an important step toward the heart. But this does not mean that all inspiring practices of our previous belief system or the texts and teachers who understand these practices are fundamentally broken and useless. We have simply moved on to a deeper exploration.

Many people I know who consider themselves SBNR *do* engage in traditions, teachings, practices, and teachers, sometimes quite seriously. There is real direction to these practices. They may no longer go to a church, mosque, or synagogue. Still, they will speak of a shaman with reverence, a mathematical equation with the certainty of an imam, a ceremonial practice with dedication and rules that they follow carefully, or a mantra practice that is exact, regular, steady, and transformational to their system.

They will adhere closely to the rules of a meditation system, saying "Oh, I practice Zen, not Metta (loving-kindness) meditation." "I practice transcendental meditation (TM), not Dzogchen." The particulars of our spiritual practice matter to us—and they should. That's because the traditions that they spring from are specific, complex, and meticulous in their ways.

These too, though not born of Eurocentric religion, and often lacking in any deity figure, are types of religious rites and practices and set almost always within strict and traditional sequence. Most practices that we turn to have a heritage. Knowing that heritage can help us if we are engaged in that practice. Lineages and heritages have power. We might think we're SBNR, but if we follow a lineage practice then we are in fact following a path with scriptures, religious viewpoints, and traditional stepping stones. If we follow a path, we should know it well so that we might see the map of the heart a bit better. If we follow a SBNR path then we might need to face the facts, and in doing so, make use of the lineage teachings, which are almost always going to be very precise and far more effective when understood more completely.

Getting Past the Postcard Aisle

We see these two problems hand-in-hand all over the map in western spiritual trends. Both problems have created huge misunderstandings and setbacks in the spiritual process of many people. They also allow us to be cultural appropriators, taking what we feel will help us and leaving the context behind.

When we are curious, when we're inspired to dig deeper, we're able to respect and revere the context and are much less likely to be an extractive spiritual tourist. These two problems make our practice surface level and stop us from progressing into stillness.

In becoming SBNR in our approach to self-inquiry we are, as I said, ignoring the fact that most of our spiritual practices do come out of a serious and organized religious context with deep roots and long lineages. It takes a long time to unpack all the information and setbacks of self-inquiry. Deep lineages are measured and tailored to individuals. They require individuals to follow a progression connected to whole worlds of other practices.

Perhaps most importantly, most spiritual practices are meant to be guided by appointed accomplished leaders in that system who have relationships with students in direct contact. It takes weeks, months, years, and decades to do certain practices within lineages that advocate for ceremony and ritual. When we divorce the practice from the context of its lineage, we can end up with misunderstood concepts and half teachings, the kind that end up on T-shirts and birthday cards. This can sometimes be playful and sweet; it can even be helpful, when sincerely applied, but it can also be so limiting that we might abandon our practice after a short period because nothing much is happening. It can stop us from integrating real work, from understanding profound concepts, and it can reduce our understanding to platitudes.

Lineage is complex and sometimes very hidden. If the heart is committed to a path, or if you are called with the strong, clear song of a tradition, become a devotee. Just that: practice dedication, self-inquiry, contentment, and absorb yourself in your spiritual community. These four balms to spiritual crisis really do work and each one is necessary.

None of us should take someone's culture and turn it into a costume. But this also goes both ways. Having genetic or ancestral claim to a tradition does not mean that your heart is committed, that you particularly like that tradition, or that you have the ability to drink reverence from its cups. We are complex. Find what keeps you honest, and be respectful—in all ways. Learn your path, and learn it well.

Tat Tvam Asi—You Are That

There is a wonderful story about a practitioner who wants to wake up to the truth of his nature. He goes from teacher to teacher, from sacred place to sacred place, looking for answers. He finally tracks down a great master and says to him, "You are famous for being wise and knowing about the truth of our nature. Please tell me, once and for all, with total clarity, the truth of my being!"

The master says to him, "Very well. The simplest teaching is the truest, and it is: *tat tvam asi*. You are that." The practitioner thinks on this for some time and says, "I don't think that's right. It doesn't really make sense." And so he leaves and continues to seek teachers and masters.

He comes across another great teacher and poses the same

question. This teacher takes a moment and then says to the practitioner, "I do know the answer. But it is very difficult to understand, and it requires much work. You will need to dedicate much time to solving this problem. You must commit sixteen years to service, working your way up in all parts of our community, cleaning, tending to things, and taking care of the space. The work is not easy and is often outright grueling. It is not for everybody. But after sixteen years, the truth will be revealed to you."

The practitioner thinks for a time and then decides, "Ok, I'll do it. I will stay here and study everything and do all the menial tasks and chores and will work toward total truth and complete understanding of my ultimate nature." And so this is what he does.

For sixteen years he works, prays, endures hardship and community sorrow, toil, and joy. As the sixteen-year mark approaches he returns to the great master and says, "Sir, you told me you would reveal the ultimate truth to me after this time. I have done the work and have studied and taken the responsibilities that you have asked of me. Please tell me once and for all, what is the truth of my nature?" The teacher looks at him and says, "Ah, yes. You're quite right. I will tell you. The truth of your nature is this: *tat tvam asi*. You are that."

The message will always be the same: we are the totality of experience. The mirror always reflects this truth. This is the universal truth. The experience of life is inside of us, not the other way around. But hearing this simple truth spoken in a short clip does not work for most people. We need to slow down and get to work to see this truth. Following the path and turning to dedication, inquiry, community, and contentment will get us there—always. Otherwise, any number of short religious statements would suffice, like "I am," "Aham," "I Am That I Am," "The kingdom of heaven is within," "The Tao that can be described is not the eternal Tao," etc. We need to be taught and opened slowly and persistently through community, practice, and commitment.

The truth of the heart is universal, but realizing and recognizing this as an embodied human being usually, except in rare cases, takes some orientation and some friends to keep us pointed in the right direction. Even when we have a direct experience of the truth of our being or hear this truth from a teacher, we may (with exceedingly rare exceptions) still need more guidance through our sticky layers. We may need to put in the work, even if the message is simple: *you are that.*

In the West, we often expect to know this information from the beginning, all at once. We want the complete manual. We want to be able to read the last page of the book whenever we feel like it, and to skip ahead or over other parts at our discretion. We resent having to do things that we do not want to do, and we want total access to everything. We can look at how we misunderstand the path itself by seeing that we have missed the context of that path. This begins to give us humility as well as curiosity. Humility and curiosity slow us down and awaken our intuition.

A Practice

1. **Notice What You Notice.** Is there a small not-good-enough voice or thought deep inside of you? Can you write down the exact words that it is whispering? This voice is the shield that covers the intuitive layer of your heart. When we can't access our intuition it's because we are bouncing off the hard shell of this small whispering thought. In order to get through this shield, we need to see the shield, listen to the voice, hear what it's saying, and then ask the voice: "Are you for real? Are you true?"
2. **Feel Your Opposites.** In order to see that this voice is not true (and I assure you this voice is not ever true), we need to see our opposites. Please write down three to five opposites that you hold in your heart simultaneously (examples might be: grief and joy, anxiety and peace, insecurity and certainty, etc.)
3. **Bow Into Yourself.** I mean this literally. Put your hands on your heart, hold your opposites, and take a long, deep bow of appreciate for how big you are. You are so big that you hold all of these

opposites. You are amazing. You are complex. You are many, many things. You are big enough for all of them.

CHAPTER 8

The Transcendence Layer

THERE IS A Zen story of two monks walking through the woods. The two monks are on a journey and returning home. One monk is a senior, and one is a novice, and both have taken stringent vows of celibacy and discipline. The two come to a river where a young woman is struggling to cross. She cannot seem to make it to the other side of the river. So, the senior monk helps her by picking her up and carrying her over the rough waters to the other shore.

Wordlessly, the two monks continue on their journey. Some time down the way, the novice turns to his teacher and says, "Sir, I must ask you—we are not supposed to speak or interact with women. It is unethical and against our vows. And yet, back there you helped a woman cross the river! Why did you do that? I don't understand. Did you break your vows? How can you justify that act?" The senior monk turned to the novice and said, "The difference between you and me is that I put the woman down on the other side of that river, and yet you are here, hours down the path, still carrying her."

We must investigate the things we hold, the stories we carry, and how we carry things. We also need to investigate our strictest disciplines, understanding the surface teachings and then the subtle teachings. We must notice how ideas keep us dragging along, heavy in our minds. In the complete spiritual path, we begin to look around and say, "I am not this. I am not that," when we are moving past the reach of the ego and toward the transcendent layer of the heart. We see: this idea does not hold me; this possession does not define me. We start to see that things are simply not what we previously thought.

Progressive Path and Direct Path

The sacred feminine and the sacred masculine need one another. There is value even in the patriarchy of religion, in measured and skillfully applied ways. Let's spend a moment doing exactly that.

There are two major forms of the transcendent pathway, both of which lead to awareness of the deep luminous void at the heart center. These are still used today, and almost universally in the seminars, conferences, study groups, and practices of self-inquiry, including both those that are religious and those that are not. I did say in the beginning that almost all of our practices for the past three thousand years have been patriarchal and transcendence driven in nature, and I meant it! We can either take the stairs up, step-by-step, to the transcendent goal, or we can take the elevator.

Usually, we follow a progression in behaviors and practices, taking a path that follows step-by-step direction toward a very certain and well-defined goal. Almost all organized religions and meditative practices fall under this approach. It is by far the most common form of inquiry, and it is called a *progressive path*. In a progressive path a teacher will take us through a program of self-realization, like the classical Ashtanga system of Patañjalian yoga, which has certain sequenced practices and a well-defined and described goal, or the Fourfold Path of Buddhism, which sets out statements about the human condition and ways to resolve our confusion. Even the simplest minfulness practices are a progressive path of bringing more awareness into the ordinary Sunday to Monday life. There are usually checkpoints, rituals, ways of showing up and practicing, and feedback from a teacher, system, or collective within this progressive path model.

The second expression of the inward path is very popular nowadays. The *direct path* is often followed by non-denominational spiritual teachers. It is sometimes called Neo-Vedanta or California Non-Duality. It's not a path without technique altogether, though, and it is important to see that. The teachers of the direct path may argue this point. However, it must be logically obvious that any time we sit with just such a teacher, we are already "practicing" and so, simply showing up (setting intention, focusing our concentration) is an action, or a step on a path.

Add to this an action, such as a form of inquiry, and now we are walking forward on that path. While people will advertise the direct path as a path without technique, there are techniques. There are simply *fewer* techniques in the direct path than there are in a progressive path. This is the elevator to transcendence approach. We are not going up the stairs, one step at a time, but instead are being asked to push just one button. The direct path may prompt us to ask just one question, like "Who am I?" rather than advocating for a series of steps or questions or rituals.

The inquiry in the direct path is precise and scientific. The teacher, usually someone who avoids honorifics or progressive path titles like "guru," scientifically dismantles the sense perceptions away from thoughts, notions of the self, sensations, and memories. The teacher brings us to a direct experience of what is happening here and now. It is an immediate realization born of investigation. There is usually just one prompt or question and then an observation period.

Dzogchen or Zen Buddhism may be two of the closest codified systems that may be described as religious that stay close to the direct path. Zen koans are single-question prompts that direct us into direct path curiosity. These are transcendent paths with more of an elevator approach. They are closer to the direct path model than some of their more elaborate sibling traditions.

Real-world observation is crucial to this model. As an exercise, a teacher might ask us to observe the sound of something "far away" like a car passing, a dog barking, or a bird chirping, and might then ask us a series of logical questions: "What is true? Can I separate that direct sound from my ability to hear? And if my ability to hear is linked inseparably from the sound, and I am experiencing hearing *here*, how can I determine that the sound is *there* or at some distance away from my axis of hearing?"

Direct path questions are one-step in nature and relentless in their focus on what can be experienced immediately, directly, and in actual time through critical observation. These questions are asked in order to collapse objects and the flow of perception into the subject. When perception stops creating a bridge between subject and object, and attention flows back into our absolute subjective awareness, we find ourselves in an inseparable experience where only our subjectivity remains.

Because the mind, including perceptions, thoughts, emotions, and sensations, are changeable, their illusory nature in both models of transcendent spirituality, the progressive and the direct paths, must be absolutely overcome as the seeker moves toward their definition of total emptiness that is fundamentally blemishless. Masculine religions call this absolute subjectivity "the soul," which is a step in the right direction, "the witness," which is closer but still alarmingly incomplete, or "undifferentiated awareness," which begins to touch the truth. In both these traditional models of liberating the individual, the student drops into emptiness, the Void, Shunya, Nirvana, the Kingdom of Heaven, or Grace, a profound experience of No Self.

It either happens step-by-step systematically or in one step immediately, but the goal is the same. The collapse of subject, perception, and object into stillness. This is why both approaches represent transcendence. Because these inward paths collapse our awareness back into our subjectivity, the other two aspects of our experience-perception and the objects of perception, are usually simply termed "unreal," and then left at that.

Jacob's Ladder

There are many ways to understand the story of the biblical patriarch Jacob's Ladder from the Book of Genesis. In a dream, Jacob saw a ladder set up on the earth that reached heavenward. On this ladder, angels were ascending and descending (Genesis 28:12). This analogy of the ladder has always struck me as a beautiful representation of the path of awakening. The angels go up *and* down the ladder, not just up to heaven. There is work to do on earth, and a steady rhythm of communication draws us alternately toward the heavenly realm or the earthly realm. Other origin stories describe a link between earth and heaven and a means to climb between realms, whether a ladder, a rope, a beanstalk, a tree of life, a world tree, or gentle wings catching someone's fall.

The subjective, the pure "I" without modifications, is like a clear sky. It is eternity and heaven. We can't quite touch it, but it is all around us, breathing and dancing us. The connection between this silent observer and the objects of the world needs some kind of connection point, some kind of organization system, some kind of ladder, whereupon we might make that journey up to the heaven of the infinite and down to the earth of difficult family arrangements, continents made of mud, and monsters lurking in the deeps.

When traveled well, this ladder brings us down into the deep, intuitive, and energetic layer of the heart. Not listening to the inner heart when it gives us information that comes on quiet, clear, little wings is deeply wounding.

In Greek mythology, when Pandora opened that fateful jar and all of the world's ills came rushing out, that small and quiet bird called "hope" (*elpsis*) stayed protected just under the jar lid. Pandora, in the stories, was the first woman created by the gods. Remember that she was also touched by the Goddess, in the form of Aphrodite, with beauty, longing, and worry.

The gods gave her intelligence, grace, a deceitful nature, persuasiveness, charm, and of course, curiosity. Like all humans—and like the gods too—she was complex. She reminds us that when the world is full of pain, chaos, and deceit, the one thing that stays protected is our hope, which points to our intuition. Hesiod's interpretation that hope is left as a means always to obey the inescapable will of Zeus belies patriarchal thinking that roundly demonizes and suppresses the female and complex movement of life. Hope, when claimed by the feminine, is instead seen as the deep call of the heart, the knowledge that things change and shift. And in us, hope is deeply protected, safe, and nourishing.

Curiosity points the light right down into ourselves and into the depths of our hearts. This task reveals the big truths that armor our hearts. But if we still carry that whisper of bias that says the transcendent is more critical or more true or more complete than the complex and mundane, then we're enacting a subtle form of stealing from ourselves, from the Goddess, from life, and from the gift of this human experience, brief and full of change as it must be.

Narcissistic Nihilism

Silence is our very nature. Awake and aware curiosity without modulations or attachments to thought, emotion, perception, body, and memory, beyond the reach of the ego, is the sacred center of our heart and this center informs all of the life that we live. It is our birthright to know this. But the ego can too easily creep in and claim this insight. If it does, if we fall in love with transcendence and deny the immanent, then we can be sure that the ego is involved, reaching its long fingers from the thought-emotion layer of our being into the deep well of the heart.

When the ego succeeds at this trick, I call it *narcissistic nihilism*. The transcendent path is essential for spiritual development, but it's incomplete. Practices that draw us inward and toward silence are good at dismantling the hold of the ego, which gives way to fully seeing and celebrating the heart.

Scraping away excess layers of attachment related to thoughts, emotions, and the body is like clearing the overgrown weeds from a patch of earth so that we can get a clear look at the quality of the soil. But we can get addicted to killing off those weeds. We can begin to think that the whole spiritual path is about cutting down and letting go, clearing out and transmuting. Narcissistic nihilism starts in earnest when we become weed whacking ninjas.

Weed whacking ninjas

One teacher I studied with had her students make lists of all the objects in their houses to see how we identify with the objects around us. This is the work on day one. On day two this then leads to making lists of the people that we know in our life, the roles that we play like sister, aunt, mother, colleague, and how we identify with those roles, and the lists continue. Her take was that everything on the list, from a dining room table to our role as a parent, sibling, or child are vines that need to get pulled back and away from the core of our being.

The upside to this teaching is that many of us do not realize just how enmeshed we are with the things of the world. We mark our self-worth by the car we drive or the brands we wear, or we mark our self-worth by whether we are a good child or a good parent or a responsible colleague. When we take a good look at these habits, we see that it is important to identify what has been distracting us, how we have given up our own awake curiosity for the accumulation of habits, objects, and roles.

The downside is that making lists of who I am not, what I am not, works just well enough as a didactic tool that it poses an addictive trap that the spiritually-minded can simply fall into.

We can swap our identification with the car we drive or the clothes we wear with our "letting go" practices. Instead of identifying with the things around us, we start to identify with the letting go of those things. We become experts. We start to take those same workshops over and over again and say to others, "I have found out the Truth! I am not what I thought I was!"

It is so freeing to drop our roles and addictions to things that the freedom is overwhelming for a time. When we become experts at a technique, we can become just as territorial over this mastery as we were previously over our identification with our car. Becoming an expert at a technique does only one thing: it makes us experts at a technique.

Hopefully, once we have written out all the items that we own or with which we identify and realize that we are not those items, the exercise has exhausted itself and we don't need to agonize over those lists again. We can stop cutting. But many of us just don't. We go back over those habits and objects like they are weeds, always needing to be cut. Constant weed-whacking, while exhilarating, is not the goal. It is another distraction. A little bit is good, it clears the paths within the city in the mirror, but too much is just more violence—internal and external.

In a best-case scenario system, once we have cut back the weeds we can get a better look at the ground. We can then turn our attention to the base of our being—to what we discover through all that hard work and self-inquiry. It is just as important to cultivate the ground of our being (Mother Earth), to nourish it with attention and curiosity, and allow the natural cultivation and growth that the earth, this being, and this body, is meant to produce.

We must allow dynamic aliveness. We must let plants grow that suit our healthy environment. Maybe some of the plants in our garden are weeds. Weeds are flowers, too, after all. But a lot of the time, we never get to a place where we can rest at the ground of our being because we are so preoccupied with cutting back. We become weed-whackers for life, never truly resting in the soil of our being and never allowing natural growth to occur and flower because we have become such great experts at the cutting process. This huge ego trap stops us from understanding our full human potential. It is the beginning of narcissistic nihilism, which is when the ego builds a new identity as a spiritual expert with a specific emphasis on the void layer of the heart.

In this new identity, we are experts at letting go, at dropping into the void, at transmuting the pain body, or at clearing negative patterns. We are experts at some method of clearing out patterns, thoughts, emotions, subtle energies, or physical distractions. We have done some amount of hard work and have become good enough at it that we think it is "the way" and therefore, we make a whole new identity of this method. The spiritual identity is as common to religious zealots as to New Age practitioners and energy healers.

What's worse is that in the subtler layers of narcissistic nihilism we have had more than a few glimpses of the ground of our being.

We've had moments of deep rest in the silence of our center. We say, "I am not this body, mind, or world." But we haven't allowed the silence to reveal its dynamic, life-giving qualities. We have sterilized the ground of our being rather than nourishing it through our awake curiosity.

Narcissistic nihilism is when we profess "nothing is real," "everything is an illusion," and "nothing exists." That is where we stop. I once went to a spiritual retreat and was sharing a meal with many deep lineage practitioners and lovers of the Goddess, and one woman at the table could not handle the chatter. She kept saying loudly to the group, "Notice the stillness that is everything" and "Let's eat in silence as that is the only truth." Later, passing through the kitchen, I thanked the same woman as she had helped to put together the dinner. She said, "Nothing happened. Nobody was doing it. Dinner wasn't made."

There is very little we can say to someone who is in a body, has a name, uses words, and engages in the activities of life, but denies that anything is happening at all. Things are happening. Life is expanding, contracting, expressing, relating, and involved. Even cooking and eating happen! At the same time, only awareness is happening. These opposites are both true, and they're true simultaneously. The silence, once seen, is a given. It is always present. It's always the ground and base and fullness of being. To have to name that silence over and over is not only redundant, but condescending. We are only signaling to others, "I know more than you do, and I am special." This can lead to real danger.

Teachers that take this stance might be caught in abusive behavior—verbally, physically, or sexually, and then say, "I didn't do those acts. Only my body and mind did those bad things, but I'm not the body and mind. I am the stillness, and since nothing is happening, there is no problem." This spiritual justification is an outcome of contraction rather than expansion. It is one where the flowers of our being are not nourished, tolerated, or allowed to perfume into the world around us. When everything is a weed then we stop seeing the flowers. We cut, and we cut, and then we show others how clean our yard is. This attitude causes grave pain in the world and in the heart.

When we claim to have a unique or entirely individual understanding of our own self-inquiry process, the best we can do is get to a place of ego isolation, which is usually called solipsism in western philosophy (Eastern models describe it well also). Solipsism is a direct product of narcissistic nihilism.

Almost all contemplative cultures have an array of warnings about the pitfalls of solipsism, which is essentially when the ego thinks, *I am One, and there is no other*. In open-hearted curiosity, infinite wisdom says, *One includes me, and all others are mirrors of the heart*. This One includes the ego. The words sound similar, but the experience could not be more different. The ego is just an inner current within the vast ocean of spaciousness, silence, creative expression, and spontaneous perception. The ego can become a healthy partner in our involution process. In solipsism, one feels isolated and lonely, standing on the shore of the ego-island and looking out into emptiness. In open curiosity, one feels expansive, compassionate, interconnected to all things, experiences, people, and occurrences, pulsating on the currents of the ego and in the infinite interchangeably.

Once again, the intention of our self-inquiry practices matters more than the practices themselves. If we are willing to drop the measurements and allow ourselves some repose, resting our focus inside ourselves, then we will experience deep transformation. But if we are stuck on willing ourselves into being better versions of ourselves, into evolving ourselves, or following a self-help track of awakening whereby we are dedicated to improving our personalities, then the best we can do is fail and see that this path did not work, making us turn back and try something new.

The deeper layers of narcissistic nihilism are truly subtle and difficult to move through, even for very seasoned spiritual seekers. Walking away does not only mean leaving family and kingdom for the ascetic path, which may or may not work out for us. We can walk away even in our own homes, never leaving the kitchen table. One direct path teacher I know, an internationally famous author and lecturer who charges a premium for her celebrity-drawing courses, sometimes tells stories about her relationship to her daughter. She will describe saying to her child, "You think you're angry with me, but you don't even exist. So whatever issue you have right now you'll have to deal with on your own because it has nothing to do with me."

I have a good friend who grew up with similar statements from her own mother—a person who was also a direct-path student, and who would constantly dismiss my friend's hurts and issues growing up from childhood through adolescence. Even now, as an adult, she will state, "That's your problem, not mine. You don't exist, so the story is unreal." Think of the years of therapy my friend has had to go through to recover from this attitude! "Go deal with that on your own because you don't exist" is said too frequently by disconnected transcendentalists who don't get it. This is not a compassionate way to honor the hearts of our loved ones, especially our children.

Now perhaps there is a level of comprehension and ego dismantling that we have personally touched where there is truth lingering in these words. But even if you have seen through the story, you can still be kind. Perhaps only when you have seen through the story can you be truly kind. We can at least acknowledge that sometimes humans, especially children, need to process with their loved ones. If we care about awakening the ones we love, then we care, too, about their heart process, all of the layers of that beautiful heart. We make efforts to walk through the mind and its play of thoughts and emotions in ways that are open and supportive, always referencing back to the heart core. If we care about our loved ones, then we care about their process as much as their goal. If we are to walk away, we must walk away from our transactions, from our preconceptions, from our superiority and knowing, but we stay present to our lives.

The way to move forward from deep transcendence, if we are attracted to life, is to absorb back into life as the full expression of the heart. Life is the enthusiastic expression of the Self. This is a beautiful word—enthusiastic—because its root is *entheos*, which in Greek means "joy in God." This is the path of absorptive recognition. It is endlessly unfolding grace. It is what most of those still-alive teachers are teaching and living.

Having free access to the place of transcendence without judging the daily noise bridges our divinity and takes us home to ourselves. The heart begins to shine forth, leading us in an open and engaged life rather than staying tucked away behind layers of pain and pattern identification.

A Practice

Notice what you notice.

1. **Practice Kindness before Honesty.** Practice kindness toward yourself and others first, always. If we go into topics like nihilistic narcissism, we are going into deep honesty. Kindness must be established before honesty to avoid slipping into violence, judgment, righteousness, and frustration. Honesty without a foundation of kindness first will always lead to violence. Practice kindness first.
2. **Journal.** With what practices do you identify most? Do you teach these practices and techniques? If you do, do you operate on the assumption that you "know more" than the people around you? This is the place to get honest and really investigate deeper patterns or assumptions of knowing better or knowing more than others. This is the time for honesty.
3. **Absorb the Energy.** It's fine to keep doing all of the work you are doing in the world. This includes leading workshops, retreats, seminars, and techniques. Doing these things is incredibly profound to people. We need not change our passions, but we must change and absorb any implicit or explicit belief that is using these practices to "set apart" ourselves or "brand" ourselves against others.

   Think of the energy of the ego. Pull up the measuring stick. Concentrate with absolute focus and open curiosity on any energy that feels bound in this way. Drop the story and just stay curious about the felt sense of the ego, as if it is a friend.

4. **Amplification Practice.** Take a core thought, emotion, or spiritual notion. Investigate this core image. Amplify it. Amplify it until you can step into it. Keep turning toward the image. The image may begin to disappear, but the amplification, the raw sense of energy, will remain. Raw energy and the image may bounce back and forth a few times, but keep amplifying. Once the story disappears, the raw energy remains. This raw energy holds a special kind of power, and we can absorb it into the heart. Rather than trying to push it away, make it bigger and stay with it. Make it so big that you can feel the power of it and enter into the power of that amplification. Step into the power as a friend, partner, or lover. Say "thank you," and let the heart open. Claim yourself.

   Know that your ego need not hold you hostage. You are friends. You can giggle together. You can cry together. You can say, "not now" or "let's play." The point is not to push away the ego here but to absorb it into the huge power of the self-reflexive heart. The ego is very small compared to the heart. The heart sees that, and it laughs.
5. **Infuse Energy with Space.** At the heart, sit with the energy you feel around this topic. See that the energy is encased, supported by, and surrounded by luminous spaciousness. Begin to slowly interpenetrate the energy that you feel with that clear, open, pure spaciousness at the heart. Where does the energy end and the heart begin? When there is no line nor distinction then the heart has begun to digest this energy. Stay with that process until you feel a deep shift, a cool vastness, or a dynamic pulsation within your heart.

PART THREE

BECOMING

CHAPTER 9

The Feminine Divine

THE INFINITE CAN be overwhelming at times, even a little blinding. Ancient peoples understood this, so when they built a house for the divine, a temple, cathedral, or synagogue, they often played with light. Sometimes they used stained glass panels to break up the light into more digestible color blocks.

The heart does the same for us. The heart takes something overwhelming and bright and it creates colorful panels through which we might see one aspect of our wholeness at a time. Every panel is beautiful and every panel represents the whole because light is light, but some of that light might be colored something like "blue" or "wise," "angry" or "a chair," or "my family."

Like the light coming through the stained-glass window, we are each whole unbroken brightness, not split or separated into pieces, though it sometimes appears that way. We can see this when we get curious and watch how the heart emits, reabsorbs, expands, contracts, creates, and destroys. Vibration works in a similar manner. Vibration pulsates, creating an expansion and a contraction. Expansion and contraction do not happen sequentially, or exclusively. Both happen simultaneously.

There is a state beyond transcendence, though it cannot be described as another layer of the heart or deeper than the transcendent layer because it is both/and. This state sees the wholeness of being simultaneously. This state is one of awakened curiosity, of softening into the musical instrument of your body that plays all of existence. When we allow the heart, instead of the mind, to play the scales of life up and down, no longer directing the ladder toward transcendence (which is essentially a mental exercise and a form of discipline), we can engage in a different, more flavorful, more engaged path of self-realization. Our path is just as limitless, just as free, pervaded by luminosity, and is astoundingly reverent and alive. Playing the scales is learning to live in freedom.

It is not a mystery that you are infinite. Enlightenment, whatever that means, is not surprising or exotic (a great word used often by Rupert Spira). It is natural and always present. What I find surprising, strange, precious, and beautiful is the fact that we exist as individuals with boundaries and uniqueness.

The individual is unique and diverse, whole in that diversity, and also the totality of being- all three. When you notice what you notice, this begins to settle in your being. The individual is never subordinate to the stillness- it is the same thing as the stillness and, if anything, its most playfully astonishing aspect.

Boundaries Revive the Wimpy Ego

Healthy boundaries are one of the most important and critical markers of the Goddess path because they are the expression of the Goddess herself. Spiritual curiosity is not about making our egos wimpy, saying yes to everything, bending when someone does something hurtful, or loving everyone and everything. Absorbing ourselves into whatever happens does not mean we need to like or perpetuate whatever happens. It doesn't mean we are not allowed to intervene. If someone starts yelling at us, it does not make us more spiritual to just take it, to go with the flow and allow ourselves to be abused. Absolutely not!

If someone starts yelling at us, then going with the flow might rightfully be to stand up for ourselves or even fight back. Being an active participant in life, allowing ourselves to flow into and through all experiences, means we do not become passive and inert. In fact, nothing about us is ever passive.

As we learned with the body, we are in constant flux and movement and change. If the body senses a pathogen, it rapidly builds defenses and tries to push out the viral or bacterial invader. That is a divine boundary. Nothing about us is immobile. Why we have come to believe that somehow our personalities must become wimpy to be truly spiritual is a mystery that I can't wrap my head around.

When we take our children to the playground and they think it's fun to pick up sand and throw it into the faces of strangers nearby, do we stand next to our children and say, "Oh, that's fine. Just go with the flow"? Of course not. We say, "Stop immediately." We give them healthy boundaries. We give them these boundaries precisely because we love them so much, not out of meanness—but out of love.

The Goddess is wise, divinely free, and also tangled up, playful, and colorful. One of the most beautiful teachings out of classical yoga found in the Bhagavad Gita is the idea of doing our work without hooking ourselves to the results of the work. This is profound. It is defined as *skill in action*. This gives us a real-world manual of how to apply the balanced and harmonious play of opposites that we express at all times. We must do our work and engage with life—we already are engaged with life! Our body is engaging and responding, and so are our thoughts and emotions.

That is not a problem. That is life unfolding. That is the dance dancing. But worrying about the result of our work—fixating on the outcome, success, or failure—is a form of holding on to something false. Worrying about the goal is how we set the stage for desire, which is the great illusion that the ego orchestrates. When we stop bartering our actions for a desired result, our work in this world is then free. My favorite passage from the Tao Te Ching expresses this same concept:

> Can you keep your crescent soul from wandering
> Can you make your breath as soft as a baby's

> Can you wipe your dark mirror free of dust
> Can you serve and govern without effort
> Can you be the female at Heaven's Gate
> Can you light the world without knowledge
> Can you give birth and nurture
> But give birth without possessing
> Raise without controlling
> This is Dark Virtue[12]

It is like that monk who crossed the river and carried his story for miles down the path. Instead of lugging around all that heavy mind baggage, the adept does a task that life puts in the path, and then puts down the task. That is the end of it. It is possible to give birth without possessing, to raise without controlling. But most of us carry that task for hours, years, or even decades: "Is what I did right? What could I have done differently? I am a bad person because I did it that way. I am a failure."

If we stop worrying about the result of our work but do our best and hold our attention steady through our movements, then these acts of violence toward ourselves and the ones we love most will naturally stop. This is the end of violence but not the end of action. Many of us can't even imagine living without the judgments, the holding of things, and the need to tally our results.

This is where the path of the Goddess begins to make sense. We can start to see what it means to go with the flow without diminishing or injuring ourselves. This means fortifying our boundaries when necessary while remaining open to a revisit of those boundaries as life shifts. It means saying no when no is safer and healthier for the heart. It means doing our work in the world or even becoming an activist, which is when we naturally turn our attention toward what our heart feels is beautiful and right. Being an activist without holding onto the results of the activism, simply showing up over and over again and doing what's possible, what can be done, may in fact be the only sane way to live.

So now let's take a look at how two different yogic traditions have portrayed the Goddess. I think you will immediately see why she looks so very different in a transcendent biased model, a limited layer of the heart, versus an embodied, both/and model that contains the whole heart.

Māyā the Trickster

"Beware of Māyā." In the classical yogic systems, the distractions of mind-stuff are sometimes personified in the Goddess form named Māyā. Māyā means illusion. She is part ego and part perception. She is beautiful, has unlimited tricks up her sleeve, and she is everywhere. She is everything that makes up the verb of the self and of life. Māyā is sneaky, and she is relentless. When we are on the inward path, she is a great trickster playing with life, making us believe that we are localized and isolated individuals and tempts us through fear and desire into the activities of thought, emotion, sensation, and the turmoil of life. She changes constantly—one thing is happening, and then another thing altogether is happening. She slips through our fingers again and again.

In western religion, direct parallels are drawn between this understanding of Māyā and the idea of evil. These traditions portray her as evil, or maybe just very problematic, and certainly not good. Because she is the conductor of illusion and always coaxing us to contract into suffering, seekers must break through, destroy, or transcend her in order to have a direct understanding of the divine. Some understand the classical path of yoga as the path of shattering and overcoming Māyā: classical yoga is the stilling or the neutralizing of the movements of the mind: *citta-vṛtti-nirodhaḥ*. It is, at its core, a path of renunciation or withdrawal from these forces. This is why letting go of the body, the last holding zone of perception and illusion, is such a high accomplishment in yoga.

Most yoga texts emphatically state that if we were to describe or explain the state of living without the illusion of Māyā, we would be attempting to describe an experience of no-self. This is an impossible task. Any description of this state would immediately lose its meaning because it would necessarily be taking on form in the act of words and ideas, thereby entering into the tricky playing field of Māyā.

This probably sounds to you like descriptions of Nirvana in Buddhism. It sounds like Samadhi or Void Consciousness in other traditions. All attempts to describe the One utilize the very movement that we are attempting to drop. So, in these traditions that consider Māyā problematic, we must follow the inward path to overcome her tricks and drop into stillness where there is no tugging, fluctuation, or action from the mind-emotion-body. We cannot even properly describe this state of transcendence without tugging at her endless strings. Words themselves must also fall away. So we are stuck, wordless, giving up a part of who we are in order to achieve the impossible.

Māyā the Beloved

From the perspective of embodied curiosity, the divine feminine loves nothing better than offering the measured back to the infinite. Seeing this brings us right into the embodied path. We do not diminish our freedom to bind, measure, or observe a thought or a sensation or a finish line in a race. But we start to see those edges within a larger picture, and we claim the limitation as an act of freedom within the fundamentally unbounded.

Paradox is when two things that are opposite and impossible to reconcile exist at the same time. This function of deep masculine and feminine is a paradox, and it is also a singularity. Limitation reveals infinity. Infinity dances as boundary, border, edge. Being in love with limitation and form, measurement and movement, is an act of wild freedom that makes love to itself, gives itself back to itself, and that need not minimize the experiences, colors, or expressions of life.

The Goddess is always laughing. She is in love with herself. She is in love with silence, her other form. She is wild and free. So much so that she puts on the costume of a thing called edges. A thing that isn't there no matter how much we try. We will fall asleep tonight and slip in between the lines. We will fall into ourselves. We will plunge in between the cracks. When we wake up, we will slip again between the lines, like the sky slips between two clouds, until the story pours in to build the world again. This is the play of total freedom.

Māyā is the beloved in tantra (she is given many names). There is a celebration, a nectar, a sweetness to life when we walk this path. The path of curiosity, the path of what it means to be self-reflexive.

There is a word in Sanskrit for self-reflection that is often used in this tradition, and it is *vimarsha*. Vimarsha is the key quality of conscious awareness—the ability of awareness to turn back and notice itself. It is a profound concept and yet it doesn't really have an equivalent in English. We don't have a word that sums up our ability to turn our awareness *back upon* ourselves. Rocks are not self-reflexive. A crystal can reflect its environment outward but it cannot look back at itself. It can emit light, it can radiate luminosity, but it cannot turn that light around and say, "I notice that light." We can because we are curious.

When we start to claim this amazing ability to notice what we notice, we begin to embrace our wholeness, power, and agency. This is the empowered path of the Goddess. This is Māyā. The Māyā of yoga and the patriarchal, only transcendent path is a very different Māyā described by classical tantra.

In the body-inclusive lineages, Māyā is one of the personifications of the Great Mother. Every representation of the goddesses is distinct in her own right and each is the totality of a whole and unbroken existence. When silence and movement collapse into one another, this perspective emerges. She, as the infinite, is the expression of life, the mother and source of manifestation, the expression of our aliveness, the beautiful one who winks at us, helps us along, tricks us as a means to encourage us, activates us, charges us, and jostles us around, but is only here to wake us up, to give us obstacles so that we might overcome those obstacles.

Māyā is both stillness and movement and, more specifically, a force that moves to reveal her stillness. Māyā is a gift because she tugs at us in a way that shows us our limitations, and if we turn toward her, we will always see those limitations.

Seeing limitations is like looking at a closed door blocking the heart. We didn't know there was a door, but now that we know the limitation, we can see the door clearly. We can see the handle of the door. We know how the hinges work. We know whether to push or pull. We can figure out how to open it. Sitting in front of that door, it will always open, revealing the heart.

A few common sayings about Māyā from this perspective include: "The poison is the nectar," "The process is the goal," and "The ground that trips us is the very same ground that holds us up." This moves us past calling her an archetype, which is limited and often prescriptive. Every obstacle in our path, every aspect of life that has appeared bitter or painful, can and must become an entry point for our curiosity according to this understanding. Māyā is still tricky, but she is beautiful, complex, mysterious, wise, and always in service to our deepest awakening. Many great mystical traditions, thinkers, and poets sing of this Goddess path.

This is the way of the mystic. The seventeenth-century saint Tukaram sums up this view by saying: "For a person who had become a true friend of the Beloved, the creepers in his courtyard are like wish-fulfilling trees. As he strolls on his way the stones on his path become wish-fulfilling jewels." The Goddess is therefore worshiped, not as an external being or entity, but as the regal divine within each and every one of us as the aspect that calls to us and turns us toward ourselves. She is living in and through our bodies as our subtle energy that calls to our heart and plays with the modifications and materials of life to help us remember that life is one whole indivisible play of awareness. Like a gem reflected in a mirror, this awareness is infused by silence but not subordinate to that silence in either truth or understanding. The gem is everywhere.

Parable of the Gem in the Forest

When we are looking for the core of ourselves, we sometimes feel as though we are searching for a beautiful gem in the center of a great forest. We think to ourselves, *As soon as I find this gem I will be whole.*

I will have completed my human journey to my heart. This gem, brilliant and hidden, calls out to us, so we start looking for it.

We take out our axes and clear a path through the thicket. We take out our broom and sweep that path to keep it tidy. This is hard work. It gets even more challenging when we soon realize that not only are we looking for this hidden gem, but all of the trees and all of the bushes and all of the objects in this vast forest are polished mirrors and fractals reflecting that gem back to us so that around every corner there it is, winking at us. It is maddening. We keep trying to clear out a path; we keep trying to sweep things away.

At some point, we begin to give up. We find a mirror or a fractal and we stop in front of it. We are exhausted. We sit and, because it's in front of us, we look at it. Little by little, we memorize the shape of the gem reflected in that tree-reflection. We look to our right and see a clear stream, and little by little we memorize the shape of the gem reflected in that water. We look to our left and see an animal, and there, too, is the gem, reflected and taking a new and surprising angle. We look down at our feet.

The path itself is the gem. We have not moved at all. We have only relaxed and gotten curious. This is the only thing that changed in the forest. When we stopped hacking around and forging forward, we just simply became curious. And they are still everywhere—those reflections. To our surprise, we see that even the ax that we've been using to clear the way is the gem. The broom we've used all along to sweep the path is the gem. The whole of the forest, far from hiding the gem, is showing it to us in every leaf, branch, bird, and pebble. It is holding out the gem to us.

The Goddess path is when every item of our awareness is the gem: not something to move past and clear away but something to approach with reverence and curiosity, absorbing us completely. We know that there will be another turn filled with new angles, that some of the peaks in the forest are free and bright and full of vistas, but some of the ravines are dark and treacherous. With our gem-broom and our gem-ax and our reverence, we walk that gem path wherever it leads. And wherever it leads, it shows itself. Once we learn to listen deeply enough to establish a continuous connection to the silent heart, we have a whole new set of choices, descriptions, and names for this integration.

Humans are really good at making simple things complicated and then developing whole systems to dig into those complications. Look at how many forms, types, practices, and rituals teach "correct" focus. In a turn of great irony, but not surprisingly, self-realization teachings fall under the complication trap just like all other teachings. The Goddess path, where everything is a mirror for our hearts, reminds us that all of these rituals and teachings are valid because they exist. Empowered with this global perspective, we choose one way forward to keep things a little easier and a little tidier, but not necessarily because it's better or faster. There are no better or faster paths in this reflective universe. There is just movement and stillness. Our awake curiosity is what reconciles, or bridges, this movement and stillness.

The full path of the heart can only happen after some moment of self-realization. After we have moved through at least some of the layers we have discussed on the inward path map of this book. We must have had some kind of expansive pause to see this path. We need a glimpse in order to recognize the whole of this path. That's ok. The good news is that you have!

This moment of self-realization is not uncommon—far from it. All people, no matter how in pain or violent or depraved, have had a moment of recognition at some point. Sometimes, the memory is hidden. Sometimes, we were young and innocent, and we brushed the experience aside, calling it something like a moment of simple joy or a moment of naive childishness. Sometimes, we do not remember this moment of absorption until a later immersion into deep beauty, peace, meditation, or in a dream. It can be hidden by a hard life, by trauma, or by the dullness of no-curiosity.

The Yoga Vasistha says:

> Even as heat is to fire, whiteness is to a conch-shell, firmness is to a mountain, liquidity to water, sweetness is to sugarcane, butter is to milk, coolness is

> to ice, brightness is to illumination, oil is to mustard seed, flow is to a river, sweetness is to honey, ornament is to gold, aroma is to a flower—the universe is to consciousness. The world exists because consciousness is: and the world is the body of consciousness. There is no division, no difference, no distinction. Hence the universe can be said to be both real and unreal: real because of the reality of consciousness which is its own reality, and unreal because the universe does not exist as a universe, independent of consciousness.[13]

Finding the Gem

One person I know turned toward the path of embodied spaciousness when she was in labor with her daughter. In the middle of the grueling and unrelenting pain, she had a moment of complete timeless expansion where every woman who had ever given birth, all of the female lineage, came to her in a moment of total clarity. The mothers said to her, "We know your mind is strong, but you can't think your way through this thing. You are ok. You have to relax. You have to let your body do this for you. Your body knows what to do. Surrender to it." This moment was a turning point and an awakening for her. The body was included. The Mother was included.

Another friend took a slower approach, investigating again and again her penchant for identifying with victimization and riding the waves of her life, which included having a narcissistic husband leave her and her baby. Every day for years, she showed up to herself, getting a little more curious, saying, *I see you, reflections in the mirrors. What is it you are teaching me today?*

Our path only really starts after we touch into what we have already known, what we have already seen: the gem is everywhere. Rupert Spira sometimes says that enlightenment (as you've seen/heard, I call this *awake curiosity*) is only the beginning. It's not the end of the book. It is simply the end of the first chapter. The rest of the book matters also. After chapter one, we are faced with the art of integrating the heart back into the world, reuniting our understanding of our global and unbound nature. Once we have reoriented our understanding of ourselves away from the complex of thoughts, emotions, sensations, and perceptions and into our ground of being, we can take that ground of being and spill it outward into those same thoughts, emotions, sensations, and perceptions. We can bring the body and all of its stuff-ness, all of its is-ness, the verb of it all, back into the infinite heart.

We can look at our ego and say, *Hello, beautiful gem. You've worked so hard to help me. You've been protecting me all along, although clumsily at times. Whenever I feel hurt you've helped me build up my armor; whenever I feel broken, you have given me the wisdom of my memory. Whisper your wisdom into my ear every now and again, old friend, but I'm in charge now of my life.*

We can sit in front of our sweeping broom with reverence. We can sit under the canopy of a mirrored tree with deep devotion. We can follow the flight of a bird overhead in awe as her wings glitter with the gem. Unless and until we claim all of life as one with the infinite divine, and yes, I do mean all of life, then we still have layers of the heart that need unpacking. The good news is that we are still walking on that glittering path, so the next scurrying thing that catches our eye will surely do just that unpacking for us.

Repose in Beauty

Beauty and philosophy have always loved one another. Some of history's wisest spiritual and philosophical teachers have talked about taking practices that draw us into clarity, depth, and peace and have even given names, tools, and practices to deepen those states. Again, we can turn to Abhinavagupta (950 CE). He acknowledges the fullness of emptiness and then looks at how exactly we can drop into these places of space—the art, if you will, of dissolving. He calls this *repose* (*viśranthi*)).

We come to rest in ourselves through an act of repose. Abhinavagupta stated that one of the highest joys was to immerse oneself in art, such as theater or poetry. Far from being an escape or an act of corruption in illusion, art, aesthetics, beauty, theater, and music were, for him, an entry point into the highest capacity of the human heart to awaken. Creative expression and beauty offer us a kind of heart practice, or so went his logic. We all intuitively lean toward creativity and art when we are expansive. When we want to dance with life, we will often do so by dancing. By painting. By putting on a costume and acting a role of great meaning or tragedy or beauty.

Art is truly a high practice, but not for the reasons we often think. It is not the catharsis of watching tragedy that pulls us back again and again. It is not the terrible movement in a powerful painting. It is not the brush stroke, the light captured, or the instrument's deep beat.

The power of art is in its ability to stop us. All pleasures invoke within us a sense of deep and expansive repose. Total rest. Catharsis, the release that happens when we immerse in an experience that allows emotional expression, is a form of leading-to-rest. Repose integrates the cathartic experience into a profound peace within that is also an expression.

If we think about it, the whole point of pleasure-seeking is to catch a glimpse or a moment of deep rest. We are looking for peace in all the pleasant acts we engage in. When we eat a great meal, we are looking for absorption into satisfaction, fullness, and rest. There is a moment where we know this pause. We often push past the pause to capture more, but nonetheless, it is that first pause we seek. In intimacy, we are looking for that moment of clarity and peace just after the immersion with the thrill of touch. Sex and touch are best when the mind stops completely. We engage in sex and touch to experience that state.

When we are sitting in a theater and experiencing the catharsis of the story through a truly great actor or production, we are allowed to drop into a state of total stillness for a time. Great music or great poetry brings us to that place, and so does working on a particularly satisfying mathematical equation or scientific experiment. At the core of all beauty is deep rest. The recognition of this does not need to take time. It's not fancy. It does not require us to do anything at all. Recognition is just noticing. The whole Recognition school of Shaiva philosophy, in the middle ages of the common era, amounted to *Notice*.

If we can expand that felt-sense of repose or stillness by gazing at art, listening to music or poetry, or sitting quietly in a theater audience, so that we habituate ourselves to the periodically available moments of clarity, then we can begin to deepen our understanding of our spacious inner nature as that clarity. We can stretch that moment of repose into several moments, like a string of pearls. If we are really dedicated, then we can enter into that flow uninterrupted for the whole duration of the experience. Many of us have done this already. We remember when we listened to that piece of music, and the experience sparkled with expansion and deep rest. We remember fondly that concert or performance, that sculpture we sat in front of for hours, being immersed in the silence of ourselves in the face of great art.

Finding rest in our wholeness is the true expression of beauty. Going by the simple name Maa, a wisdom teacher of Śrī Vidyā once used these words: "Beauty is that which harmonizes higher states of consciousness with lower states. Universal and relative. Mundane and divine. Beauty is that which stops the mind. Beauty can dissolve the fragmented and inauthentic sense of the self. It stops taking or objectifying the world and just looking at 'what does it mean to me'; beauty expounds it and lets it be. Beauty doesn't make it an object but allows it to be what it is." These words show us why we are so attracted to beauty and give us the heart's perspective on what it calls beautiful—that which creates deep rest, deep wholeness.

This repose does not need to be fleeting or connected to a song or artist or meal. It is possible to lean into the repose itself so that we no longer need to look for that moment of fullness. We can spill the recognition on either side of the experience until the experience itself is like a boat bobbing on the waters of deep repose. We can approach all experiences in the spirit of artful repose so that satisfaction can expand around them, instead of being reserved for a fleeting moment. We can drop in through the whole concert, the theater production, and the experience of entering the museum to find the painting that calls to us, so the moment of repose does not begin and end at satisfaction or beauty but pours forth in the whole act of turning toward art.

The Luminous Heart

When we point to ourselves, we point to our chest as if to say—*my heart is me*. We do not point to our heads. The mind is chatty, but the heart is quiet. It is absolute silence, or, in the words of T.S. Eliot, the "Still point at the center of the turning world." The heart is too busy listening to life, pulsating with all-that-is to make a noise.

When we look at the anatomy of the heart, we pivot around this place of stillness at its center. The body, thoughts, emotions, and intuitive power that lead to the heart's center lead to this silent ocean of energy. Because the heart center is so silent yet powerful and full, the turn toward the heart is a natural path for most wisdom traditions. Because this heart is still and intuitive, referenced by almost every culture and tradition in human history, the body is truly the living and moving temple that holds the gem of stillness that is singularity in the center of each of us. Even physics uses the term singularity. In the scientific model, it is the singularity from which the universe emerges within each one of us no matter our physical location in space. Stillness, singularity, is the point from which everything expands and everything contracts.

Some part of us understands that there's stability at the heart, a kind of core I-am-ness that holds its integrity even when the turnings of mind, body, thought, emotion, and sensation revolve around it—never able to touch. Many, if not all, classical teachers and practitioners of self-inquiry turn to the divine silence within the individual at the heart. A silence that, it turns out, is in fact the ground of everything, including that individual. This is the heart of embodied awareness. It is the seat of repose.

This silence is not sterile or static. It is a silence that pulsates like a heartbeat. It is dynamic. For every religious tradition that has turned inward in silence, many fringe, mystical adepts have spilled over the edges of their organized faiths, turning back outward in song and praise of that very same silence that moves as life. They see the dynamic flavor of silence. These are not different paths but rather different perspectives and progressions of the one path of the divine—the one goes toward the center of the no-self, and the other moves from the center of the no-self or void outward as vibration, sound, movement, and form.

I once was in an argument with my husband and he was particularly annoyed. He finally said in exasperation, "You're being so unpresent! Maybe you just need to be more present!" What he wanted was for me to get more spacious and quiet. I promptly replied, "And maybe you should be *less* present!"

Sometimes, we need to be engaged in our process rather than set apart from it. This is one way of being accountable. I know many people who believe they need to figure themselves out before entering a relationship. *I want to date myself for a while* or *I should get to know myself first before I date someone else.* This is beautiful. But going into an intimate relationship means going into a process, and dynamic process at that. We do get to know ourselves through that mirror of the lover. Relationships show us our colors and open whole doorways to our inner hiding places, lies, and agendas.

My husband would like to be quiet, earthy, and steady. I, on the other hand, do best when working with a full rainbow of emotional expression and a large canvas. Our partners are our first and best mirrors to our patterns. We will inevitably discover that that dynamic mirror can be both disquieting and profoundly liberating when we look closely at what bounces off the mirror and back into our consciousness.

The key to moving through emotions is to stay with them—boldly and with fortitude as well as curiosity. This is getting present.

Sometimes, this means allowing the emotional state to move through its entire course without reacting, without trying to suppress or limit the feelings, and then investigating those feelings fully once the wave has washed through. Every response and reaction reflects a thought, emotion, or memory that is undigested at the heart.

Emotion takes us away from silence but it does not make the moment less present. Instead of saying, *I need to be more present*, we might say, *Let me feel this whole story in real-time, while I'm feeling it, and allow this flavor of presence to deepen me into my heart because there is a wound here, there is older material here.* If we are particularly reactive and have a deep wound, then we may want to have our process with a therapist or write it down. We might want to take a look inward before involving the other.

If we do not know what emotion we are sparking, then we might take this practice a step further and do the exact opposite of let it go. We might turn toward our feelings and amplify them. Amplifying means going a bit deeper, within a safe space, and through conscious and heart-connected practice to touch the inner walls of our true feelings and allow those feelings to open up and decompress.

Spiritual stickiness is simply a part of the self-inquiry process. When we see it in ourselves and within our loved ones and teachers, we see an arrow in neon lights pointing to a deeper thought, memory, or suppressed assumption that remains unrecognized. Watch it. Catch it. Stay with yourself. Don't jump forward. Don't suppress it or disassociate.

We can get skillful enough to explore past that certain growth edge that catches us in a tailspin and have insight as well as find challenges in new and uncomfortable ways. We can allow and digest the darkness, the process, the dance of the curious path so that it guides us as well as the light, and we can get better at sniffing out our discomfort when it shows up small and distant in our field. We can deepen our perception. We can wake up to the unimaginable miracle and beauty that is the whole of our being, exactly as we are. This happens when we fully meet as the deeper thoughts—those core roots that sprout upwards and outwards as emotions, thoughts, and reactions.

When we can meet our deeper prejudices, we can find more generosity for ourselves and others because we claim our own impressions and patterns, which means that what's out there does not need to change. The change happens *in here*. This gives us sovereignty and takes pressure off the world to adapt to our hidden expectations.

Beige-Washing Our Feelings

Think of how profound this statement is: I am allowed to feel my feelings. Isn't it amazing how deeply we project our spiritual ideals of being quiet and being peaceful onto ourselves and others? This ego trap reflects what can happen if we cultivate a wimpy ego.

This ego trap reminds us that feeling the full range of human feelings is natural. Dr. Richard Miller calls this "welcoming." Feeling, sensing, and emoting are facts of life, but most of the time we don't welcome our feelings. We just kind of put up with them and hope that they go away, or we try hard to get them to go away, or we suppress and disassociate and pretend that they are not there at all.

Spiritual beige washing sometimes says, *You should be quiet; you should be peaceful.* Or, *I need to get through this horrible no-good phase so that I can be quiet so that I can be peaceful.* Inner peace cannot be shaken, like a deep sea in a storm; it reveals itself as the ground of our being. We are an ocean of silence with currents and movements that we call thoughts or sensations or perceptions. But we don't need to work for that understanding as though it is something we don't know—something to get to.

Sometimes something global will rock us to our core, especially an injustice or a war. I was swept sideways by a global conflict once and spent several weeks untethered. One night, a few weeks into this agony, when simply checking to see if I had gotten some water for my bedside table, my husband asked, "Do you have everything you need?" He was only asking me about water, but I heard his question globally, with my whole heart. I took a few moments and then said, "Yes, actually, I do have everything I need."

I was able to recognize my inner peace without diminishing the sadness I was feeling. It doesn't seem possible that we can hold total peace as well as infinite movement, but it is possible and a remarkable insight to absorb. It is almost as though life is always upleveling us, asking, *Can you find peace here, too?* But it's a trick question. The answer is always yes, but not without a good amount of work, a willingness to access tears and grief, and an ability to drag ourselves forward and show up always for ourselves.

Here we are claiming: feel what you feel. Notice what you notice—you should be practiced at this now! It's self-reflexivity that we are celebrating, the curiosity, in this practice, which is already full with itself. Curiosity does not care if feelings are bright or dull, if the waves are big or small. It simply shines with the light of its own noticing. We do not deny what we sense in this radical path of awakening. Both peace and movement are acceptable here. Both arise within the infinite ocean of awareness and are awareness. Worrying about what appears in our awareness is like worrying about what color we choose to paint a canvas in front of us. Any color will leave a mark. All marks will appear on the canvas. The canvas will accept all colors without discrimination or protest. We are trying to notice the canvas, not the color on it.

Of all the great traps, this particular ego trap is the one that catches me again and again. I will have a moment of emotion or reaction—I will feel sad about something or confused or frustrated, and I will feel that the response is too big, too bright, too emotive. I will immediately try to beige-wash my feelings. I will try to rush through the process or I'll whisper, *No, you're not welcome here!* When deep repose and recognition meet resistance, it somehow changes the entire landscape. This does not permit us to be wild and violent, only to see that there are reds and blues in our experiences too.

It means allowing what appears without asking it to be something else. Without saying to it, *Tone yourself down. You're too much.* When we allow our wholeness, reactions do quiet and calm dramatically because they don't need to shout to get our attention. Then, emotion can signal, and we turn with full attention. That is indeed an art and a sign of deep heart practice.

▼ ▼ ▼

A Practice

1. **Remember Repose.** Contemplate a moment of deep expansion that you experienced. If you've experienced many, choose the one that's most present and potent in your memory. If you can't remember any moment of deep expansion, then get curious. There are moments there, and many of them. It may take some time to recall them. A memory may come to you in a dream or in that in-between place between dream and sleep. When you recall the memory, write it down. Was there a moment of deep repose? Where did you perceive your edges in that moment, and was there any movement in your heart? What was that like for you?
2. **Find Repose Now.** Pull up your favorite form of art or aesthetics. A song. A painting. Something that you love. Sit in a posture of conscious repose. Keep your attention on the stillness of your heart rather than on the movement of the form. Keep your attention inward even as it is allowed to flow outward. Do both, lightly.
3. The Buddha was once asked by a famous musician, a sitar player, "How do I cultivate this stillness in my music? Do I do this before I play or while I play?" The Buddha asked him, "When you tune your instrument in preparation to play, what do you do?" The musician said, "I turn the strings so that they are not too tight and not too loose. That way they vibrate the best." The Buddha replied, "This is just how your attention should be: when you are playing keep your attention soft, not too focused on the flow of the music and not too focused on the internal state of stillness. Keep your attention in the middle, holding both so that you are not too tight and not too loose." This is called the Middle Way. When we pay attention to deep beauty, when we engage, we can follow this Middle Way, just like the Buddha taught.

CHAPTER 10

Relationships that Matter

ONE OF THE most famous teachers in the history of Buddhism was a tenth-century Tibetan adept named Marpa, the great teacher of Milarepa. Marpa stands out in the stories because he maintained a family, wife, and sons despite being an exalted teacher. When his beloved son (and lineage successor) died in a horseback riding accident, Marpa was openly devastated. His students were perplexed and asked him, "You teach us that life is a dream, an illusion, that death is natural and everything is impermanent, and that attachments are unreal. Why do you weep for your son?" He replied, "Yes, everything is a dream, but the death of a child is like a nightmare in the dream, a super-illusion among illusions. Nothing is more painful than that." His ability to cry, drop into despair, and feel human feelings was a lesson to those in his time who engaged in beige-washing their experiences. It is a lesson for us today.

Let's Talk about Sex

We can't talk about the power of relationships and holding space for each other without talking about sex. Relationships are the most fabulous artistic creations we express—relationships to other humans, to the earth, to our inner process. Intimate relationship is one of the places of our most profound recognition and one of the places of our most hidden pain and indulgent heart armoring. It is so sad that we live in a culture that glorifies promiscuity, as though sex is something to acquire or an experience to trade.

Yet, this is how popular culture advertises sex. Every episode of the show brings in a new partner, a new drama. After ten or fifteen sexual partners, the season ends, only to begin again the next time around.

It makes sense that we needed to make our sexual freedom visible after millennia of repression. Arguably, the patriarchal system of religion initiated by the priests of the ancient Israelites (told about in the Bible) was an attempt at limiting the sexual freedom of women to shift from pre-Bronze age matrilineal systems, where family lines passed from woman to daughter to a patrilineal system, where property and possessions passed from father to son. As I mentioned in Part One, societies in what is called Old Europe, the regions of Europe, Anatolia, and northern India before the common written language, honored the Goddess. Part of this reverence likely included sexual freedom and sacred sex for women, especially within the temple. Women bore the children, and so, logically, lineages passed through the mother.

When monotheistic religion moved to patriarchy, it did so by routinely and savagely creating systems of terror, abuse, and disempowerment for all women. Many Bible passages imply that the free sexual practices associated with Goddess worship were a primary target of male authority, where men desired to have assurance around the paternity of their children. This campaign against women lasted for at least two thousand years. We see it referenced in stories of Goddess cults from the earliest Bible passages to Christian zealots commenting well into the fourth and fifth centuries of the common era, until Christianity suppressed the last of the Goddess temples in those centuries.

Four thousand years of systemic repression of female sexuality, often brutally executed, need to be reckoned and healed person by person, household by household. Modern women are doing this. But swinging the pendulum to transactional sex and keeping it there in culture has not helped us deepen into our hearts.

The women of the Goddess temples did engage in natural sexual freedom. The children born to these sacred women were celebrated (rather than called "bastards" or rejected), but remember that this sexual freedom was a response to the sacred and life-giving qualities of nature and the divine feminine and grew out of cultures that took it as a given truth that women are whole, complete, divine, and worthy.

You and I live in a time of whiplash where we went from centuries of deep sexual repression, millennia of men owning women in all colonized places on the globe, to wild irreverence and sexual experimentation in one or two generations. In current times, we are more frequently than not still acting out in our sexual conquests, especially women, in an attempt to soothe the rage and grief that thousands of years of patriarchy have printed into our ancestral and genetic memory.

Both of these expressions, repression and sexual rage, are extreme and unbalanced. Having said that, there are still places where this revolution has not happened and where it is overdue. These are places where the plain fact that women have sex and have miraculous, pleasure-seeking, life-fulfilling and life-giving bodies is still systemically and brutally oppressed.

It is time to look at sex and partnership with freedom, curiosity, and the reverence it so profoundly deserves. We need to uplevel our understanding of this most basic human act into the self-reflexive path of the heart. After we habituate into clarity and rest in beauty, wherever we express that, we can expand that state to fill an ever-greater lens of our lived experience. Maybe we can engage in touch, sex, and partnership so thoroughly that touch becomes an expression of living, unfolding repose based on curiosity and reverence. An expression of stillness dancing. Of the human interfacing with the divine, the body with the heart. Then, as the repose saturates and amplifies, all interaction, conversation, argument, or exchange with our loved ones can be enveloped in that repose.

Sex with an intimate partner (or partners) can then become an act of prayer, a visit to a temple, instead of an impulse of acquisition. We must be adults, and we must value ourselves as whole and divine to meet such a partner sexually. Too often, when we have not healed our ancestral and collective shame, the drama of multiple partners becomes an expression of insecurity and teases us with this possibility: *Is there someone out there who can meet me in my wholeness, who will love me completely for the way that I am? Can that person stay exciting to me and can I be enough for them through the long slog of years and decades. Can they stay open to the changes in my body, emotions, thoughts, and dreams? Can we play the edge of life and death together? Can we play the edge of boundlessness and limitation in every interaction together?*

Basically, we are asking our intimate partners, *Are you enough for me? Am I enough for you?* If the answer is yes, then we likely no longer want to practice liberating promiscuity, with some exceptions for those with serious dedication and integrity. We usually have plenty of material to stay and explore this foundation, this dance of edges and the infinite, in partnership of two. Human intimacy is full-time devotion. Once we see that we are enough, we enter into clarity. We interact with people transactionally or from the heart.

When we see this in the most intimate parts of our lives—in sex and relationships—we come to understand that everyone is a reflection of the deep heart. We are hungry to know each other. Everyone we meet, whether we're looking for a sexual experience or a friend or even a comfortable hello, we're asking them in some subtle way, *Can you love me?*

We are attracted or repelled by people based on this subtle inquiry, and depending on our traumas and deep patterns, we may be attracted to those who we feel can love us in wholeness or those who cannot. We know immediately and somatically whether the one standing in front of us is capable of total love, partial love, or neglect. We make decisions based on this expansion or contraction. When we enter into agreements with people, whether sexual or cordial, we know the outcome intuitively and from the first moment.

Some partnerships based on transaction and contraction last a very long time, and in most marriages where the patriarchy rules, this can be subtle or overt. This is when one partner might eventually say to another, "Don't touch me." Sex can be weaponized and used as a reward or punishment. This is only possible when patriarchal values have climbed into the marital bed. Sex then becomes power and can go from being the carrot, *Do this thing and we can have sex*, to the stick, *You didn't do this thing, so you don't get it.*

The problem is not sex. Transaction is a function of the mind, not the body. But it's easier to complain to our friends about sex than to say to ourselves or others, *I don't feel like my heart is being seen. I can't figure out how to see my partner's heart. Until I feel like a whole person in my eyes and their eyes, I can't enter the temple of intimacy because the ground is too cluttered. I need to figure out how to sweep the temple first, but I need help.*

Cleaning the Temple

Sometimes we need to shape up our patterns so that we can be healthy at a human level. This is what I mean by cleaning the temple. Now, let me reiterate: If you no longer identify as human in your process of self-realization, then nothing in this section, let alone the book, is of any use. We are humans, remembering ourselves as whole. And every mystical tradition says that the human realm is where awakening can happen.

The Bhagavad Gita goes so far as to claim that the gods and celestial beings are themselves subject to birth, death, and rebirth. Self-realization cannot happen on the divine plane—it's just too easy to coast along in paradise without any activations as sandpaper to scratch at us. The analogy holds a beautiful point. The things that rub us the wrong way are gifts. We are like little pebbles being smoothed over again and again by the river of life. Sometimes a lesson feels like a gentle wave passing over, and sometimes, we feel like we're being tossed in storms. Either way, we are being polished.

My daughter went through a phase where she loved to watch shows about keeping a tidy home. We all had to get on board and spent more than a few rainy days cleaning up our house. We learned to fold and clean out the cabinets (and the junk drawers!), and we figured out how to organize our pantry systems so that we knew what we were working with when we needed to make a meal.

Households have always maintained pride in tidiness. People the world over sweep their floors, whether the ground is humble earth or tile or wood or rock. In some cultures, women learn to catch their babies in childbirth so that the child never touches the floor, which might be dirty or unsafe. When we walk into a cluttered space, we feel like something is deeply wrong or even risky.

Our interior space is just like this. All of the practices in this book and all of the stories about methods of concentration, meditation, and mindfulness are ways that we sweep the floor of our inner temple. We need to know where our patterns live and we need to know where the cobwebs grow—the places we don't want to go. I've talked about this in different ways, but now we need to see just how relationships can help us both in cleaning our temple and in keeping it clean.

In terms of cleaning our temple, our friends, partners, allies, and teachers can hold the space for us to see inside a bit better. It's like they are standing at the doorways holding flashlights. We want this help. It is sacred work. It's important that these helpers are there when we need them and that they know how to gracefully walk away once that room is clean. It is said that when the student is ready the teacher will appear. It is also said that when the student is really ready, the teacher will then disappear.

Keeping the temple clean is a slower and deeper process. Once the ego has been seen, once the measuring stick is our sweet but sometimes annoying friend, once our triggers are welcomed and investigated, life moves a bit more freely. We give up the rigid "me" and become the complex "I." We flow with ourselves. We flow with life. Flow means the wind might just pick up some dust and brush it over our temple floor. That's ok. If we are in enlightened partnership, our partner might see this happening before we see it ourselves.

To be curiously open in a relationship means to agree to these sacred terms: *My greatest wish is to support you in your waking up process, and I know that your greatest wish is to support me in mine.* At the highest level, this is why we enter into deep romantic relationships or the highest spiritual friendships.

As humans, it is natural for us to fall in love with the clear mirror that reflects us to our beloved and that reflects them back to us. Once, I was going through a rough patch with my husband and I finally said to him, "Look, I don't care about a traditional set-up here. I could take or leave what society says about our roles and why it matters that we're doing this thing. The kids are fine and they will be fine because we love them. But this is between you and me. The only thing I care about is agreeing that we are here to reflect each other. I want you to wish only for my awakening and I want you to trust that I only wish for yours. This means if you say or do something out of pattern I will call you out on it, lovingly but quickly, and I will trust you to do the same. Otherwise, it makes no sense to me to have this thing called human marriage."

I did not know if he would agree. I knew that I was putting it all out in the open, and I knew it was risky, especially since he does not follow any kind of traditional spiritual practice. But he did agree. And this is now the core of our relationship. We have our stumbling days when we miscommunicate or our egos get involved. When that happens one of us will say, "Do you want to talk about it?" This is what it means to keep the temple clean. We leave the door open to the flow. If the dust blows in, one of us will see it right away and address it. We want to keep each other's temples clean. This is our sacred agreement.

The Culmination of Practice

If I were to find a bracelet among my family items, I would bring it to a competent and skillful jeweler and ask, "What is this made out of?" I would trust that the jeweler has the skills, tools, techniques, and measurements to determine the answer. The jeweler might say, "I need to investigate and test this material. I need to run it under a solution. I need to peer at it closely through the microscope. I need to touch, bend, and bring it close to my eyes and senses." These are the skills, and the empowered means that the adept has—that they have done over and over again to develop clarity, power, and confidence.

Once the jeweler says, "Ah, this bracelet is gold," then the techniques are no longer necessary. The empowered means, the skills, tools, and techniques are not needed. The jeweler doesn't need to subject the bracelet to another test. The jeweler doesn't need another microscope, solution, hammer, chisel, or light. Once gold is seen for what it is, we no longer need to test it. This is the end of practice. Gold is gold. I don't need to test this material again to know what it is, because I already know.

Spiritual practice tests the gold of reality. In all spiritual means, we ask one question: "Who am I?" We test our reality over and over again. We do not rely on the words of other people. We are investigating our minds, our hearts, our thoughts, our emotions, our body. The skills take time to develop. We must get quiet. We must get organized. We must know how to read our studies to avoid bias in the investigation.

The Buddha said,

> O bhikshus and the wise,
> Just as a goldsmith tests his gold
> By burning, cutting and rubbing it,
> So you must examine my words
> And accept them,
> But not merely out of reverence.[14]

Once we see reality for what it is, once gold is gold, the testing is no longer important. We do not need to investigate ourselves to ask, *What is this? Who am I?* We can put down the telescope. We can put down the practice. This marks the end of the transcendent path.

This is not the end of spiritual development for us because we are not only the jeweler; we are not only the investigators looking for answers; we are also the client asking the questions and the one who puts on the jewelry, delighting at how we sparkle and shimmer. Indeed, once we see that gold is gold, then the fun begins. Instead of looking and testing, we can now trust the material. We know what we're working with. Awareness is awareness. Life is life. Now we can take that gold and make something with it.

Perhaps we would like to take our bracelet and leave it alone—put it on our wrist and admire it. Perhaps we'd like to take that gold and melt it, burn it, scrape, bend, pound, and shape it. Perhaps we'd like to make that gold something wild. Maybe we want a necklace. Maybe we want a delicate anklet with bells that ring when we walk, we can hear ourselves jangle, tinkle, and dance with every step. What we do with the practice after we understand what we are, who we are, what we are not, and who we are not, is where the fun lies in the spiritual path. It is where we can adorn ourselves in the gorgeous beauty of awareness. We can drape ourselves with awareness. We no longer need to test the awareness, but that does not make the awareness less fascinating, less beautiful, or less ornamental.

If anything, now that we have taken away the microscope, we might be able to saunter out of our house draped in gold. We might spin it into our hair, into our clothes. We might shine that gold through our eyes. If anything, we might now make use of the gold to bring beauty to the world. We do not often think about this part of spiritual understanding. It's time to fashion ourselves and adorn ourselves with the beauty of the practice.

There is a deep purpose to the path of the heart, which is singular. It will always return to itself. Purpose is something that I think is misunderstood in spiritual circles. There is only one higher purpose no matter what path or story it takes: to break through the patterns and limitations of the mind and live through, as and with the many layers of the heart, and to allow our open curiosity to get us there. The heart is the calling of the deep self as pure awareness.

The heart is the place that knows peace because *it is peace*, both in stillness and in dynamic expansion and contraction. This paradox must be understood and accepted at a level the mind cannot comprehend. The heart is always the reorientation, path, and goal. And the language that the heart uses to remember itself can be vast: pleasant, painful, terrorizing, agitating, and joyful in turns.

Opposites play together—pleasure and pain, expansion and contraction, ease and grit, to bring us there. After all, this is the blueprint: expand, contract. What is amazing is how universal the heart is in that singular pulsation. At the same time, the way that each of us returns to this understanding is unique. Our path should not be the same as our neighbor's or our teacher's. The knowledge that comes from the heart is universal, but the way there is our own. Chögyam Trungpa says, "When you receive spiritual instruction from the hands of another, you do not take it uncritically, but you burn it, you hammer it, you beat it, until the bright, dignified color of gold appears.... It is not enough to imitate your master or guru; you are not trying to become a replica of your teacher. The teachings are an individual personal experience, right down to the present holder of the doctrine."[15]

We've seen how activations are a specific language used by the heart that we must take seriously. Our activations burn, hammer, and beat our knowledge so that we can absorb the teachings that bring us home. They are the mirrors that reflect the armoring of our hearts on any and all levels of our being. When we miss one, we will receive another from a different place. This is why our patterns feel like they're unique to us: that same pattern coming up again and again. That thing that seems to happen to us over and over but not to our friends or relatives. This is the heart of plain honesty, responsibility for ourselves and our actions, and recognition of every small pang of pain—a sure sign that this activation must be followed relentlessly to its core to be seen and understood. The path of the heart requires that we pay the tolls in many small acts of courage and fortitude.

Now, as you go on your path, remember there are deep canyons of love. In the Tao it is said that the ocean is more powerful than the rushing river because it is lower than that river. We must be lower than ourselves to express our power. This is a great teaching on the power of humility, but it is also much bigger than humility. It is in the lower places that we hold, we find depth, we find our largeness. Movement flows downward with gravity, where it collects and magnifies.

Many of the lessons that I have learned in my process have uncovered layers of painful spiritual arrogance, markers of desire like anticipation, anxiety, nostalgia, and shame. These are ways I have protected myself. These are ways I have held my heart back, cloaked myself, and hidden from the terror and discomfort of my process. These are the rushing rivers that have caught my attention and that I've repeatedly jumped into to drop down into the ocean of the heart.

A friend said to me once: "Nothing is special; everything is sacred." My response was—wow—you just summarized the whole path. This is the description of faith. We take out the comparisons. We remove the flashing experiences. The rushing rivers drop into the vast, quiet, deep and whole sea. That is where heart-faith can be truly saturated.

We can get low enough, quiet enough, to look around and say: "Everything is sacred." Enlightenment is not a special state. Really, enlightenment does not exist. There is simply no such thing. For enlightenment to exist, there must be a hierarchy. For enlightenment to exist, there must be something called not-enlightenment. Fancy experiences of the divine can come and go, like all experiences. Every fully self-realized teacher will tell you that enlightenment is just a word used to describe ordinary life where everything is reverent and extraordinarily sacred.

The intelligent mind is not the mind that is good at memorizing, at cutting up the world and describing it, at using logic and reason and argument and persuasion. This is how intelligence has typically been described and taught to us. It is a limited model. The intelligent mind is not the mind that's good at math, science, or literature by holding onto facts or stories or memories, despite what school and society tells us. That's just a mind good at climbing up and down the measuring stick. The best this type of intelligence can do is become master of something.

The mind of the Goddess in you moves through learned skills and begins to develop intuition, wisdom, and wholeness, abandoning the reliance on memory, comparison, and judgment. Real intelligence looks like wisdom. Acquisition of facts can happen in wisdom or not. Some people like facts (like Hermione). Some people do not. It just does not matter. Intelligence is responding openly and creatively to the freshness of the moment from a place of wholeness.

Every path leads to devotion. We are either fueling compulsion or dropping into reverence.

Let me share an open secret with you: At some point, your reverence will bloom so big that you will stop worrying about what the mind says, what the body does, or whether you are climbing the measuring stick. At some point, you begin to see that everything you've ever done has been an act of reverence. At some point, you receive the reverence instead of trying to reach for it or act upon it. You no longer move toward it. It pours into you.

You become the receptacle for life so you can pour that reverence back out to life in a simultaneous give-take dance. You see that reverence is all there is, regardless of how you have perceived it or how the world perceives it.

Remember now that all things are made of curiosity, or awareness, or consciousness. All things are infinite and unbroken. The divine game is learning to marvel at the limitations, the wild strangeness, the impossible dance of this beautiful life. May you dance it.

Notes

1 Maurice Frydman, *I Am That: Talks with Sri Nisargadatta Majaraj* (Acorn Press, 1973), 125.

2 Sophus Helle, *Enheduana: The Complete Poems of the World's First Author* (Yale University Press, 2024), 63.

3 Halle Iglehart Austen. *The Heart of the Goddess: Art, Myth and Meditations of the World's Sacred Feminine* (Monkfish Book Publishing, 2018).

4 Halle Iglehart Austen. *The Heart of the Goddess: Art, Myth and Meditations of the World's Sacred Feminine* (Monkfish Book Publishing, 2018), 4.

5 Jeffrey J. Kripal, "Remembering Ourselves: On Some Coutnercultural Echoes of Contemporary Tantric Studies," *Religions of South Asia* 1.1 (2007): 13.

6 Ṛg-Veda X.125.3-4/8.

7 Andrew O. Fort and Patricia Y. Mumme, *Living Liberation in Hindu Thought* (State University of New York Press, 1996), 198. Excerpt from Abhinavagupta, trans. Paul Muller Ortega.

8 See *Īśvarapratyabhijñā-Kārikā* by Utpaladeva and *Tantrāloka* (ch. 3) by Abhinavagupta (c. 850-950 CE).

9 Bessel van der Kolk, MD, *The Body Keeps the Score: Brain, Mind, and Body in the Healing of Trauma* (Penguin Books, 2014), 316.

10 Bessel van der Kolk, *The Body Keeps the Score*, 333.

11 *Tantrāloka* 13.140-141.

12 Red Pine, *Lao-Tzu's Taoteching* (Copper Canyon Press, 2009), 20.

13 *Yoga Vasistha* III:14 (On Creation).
14 From the Ghanavyuha Sutra.
15 Chögyam Trungpa, Cutting Through Spiritual Materialism (Shambhala Publications, 1973), 19.

Acknowledgments

There are many doors that lead back to the heart. I thank each and every one of them. To my teachers, who have been many in number, and often pioneering women in their worlds. Of these I count Jazmin Lieb, my first yoga mentor; Bonne Greenwell, who was studying Kundalini Awakenings and embodied non-duality before most people had heard of the terms; Sally Kempton, whose very being could transport and who advised me through very important recognitions that allowed my heart to interface with the world- with breath and humility. Many years studying with Rupert Spira and other non-duality teachers allowed me to see the ordinary as extraordinary. Giving birth to two children connected me to a love that I did not know was possible, dangerous and unquestioning and connected to bodies that need the earth, and that in an instant connected me to the countless mothers who are nameless in my own body's history. They held and loved and did not need to be remembered beyond that simple need. To the tormenting energy that threw me into the infinite and demanded that I hold a very human life- the Goddess herself. To my teacher, Sravana Borkataky-Varma, who told me to put on a dress nearly the first time I met her and who keeps me practicing. To my Tantra teachers, especially Ben Williams, who can make thousand-year-old texts feel more exciting than the latest album drop. To my sisters, especially my twin who regularly trains me in honesty. To my parents. To my soul friends. To my husband, who is the steady ground to the wild bird of my spirit. To life. Life is the pulsation of the breath. Fortunately, if we forget it, it simply comes again- and again. So above all, I acknowledge my breath and that moment—who can say if it was in time—when the breath became Mother and remembered herself if only for the thrill of giving herself back to herself again and again. And, since you've been patient, I'll cut to the chase: to You—to your expressions, your bravery, the stories you have held, and mostly to your curiosity. Thank you.

Cynthia Abulafia is part of a tantric shakta lineage. She has spent most of her adult life studying the goddess figure in archeology, religion, and psychology. She is also currently in the master's program on Yogic Studies at Naropa University. Already she has the highest teaching credentials in yoga, including 500 E-RYT, YACEP, C-IAYT (Yoga Therapy) and others. She has taught yoga, yoga therapy, and trauma informed movement for over 20 years, and is a lead teacher trainer at Yoga Soup in Santa Barbara. She holds a master's degree in nutrition (MSNE). She lives in Santa Barbara, CA.

MONKFISH
BOOK PUBLISHING COMPANY

We are
Monkfish Book Publishing

...an independent press publishing spiritual and literary books from a diverse range of perspectives. Genres include memoirs, wisdom literature, fiction, and scholarly works of thought. Monkfish books appeal to the seasoned or novice seeker as well as to the general public looking for reliable sources on spirituality. The readers we had in mind when we began Monkfish in 2002 were devoted spiritual seekers, the type whose passion for the spiritual quest would lead them to read across a dazzling array of traditions: Buddhist, Hindu, Jewish, Christian, Muslim, Native American and more. It has always been our intent to publish works of spiritual authenticity for the general public as well as the specialist and scholar.

Our books are available from booksellers everywhere.

Use this QR code to see recently published books:

Use this one to sign-up for our monthly newsletter:

www.ingramcontent.com/pod-product-compliance
Lightning Source LLC
Jackson TN
JSHW070357121225
94898JS00001B/1